Inner Child Healing

A Guide To Greater Awareness Through
Reparenting The Lost Inner Child

Damian Blair

Disclaimer

Inner Child Healing
First edition. October 9, 2021
Copyright © 2021 Damian Blair

Cover image under license from Shutterstock

Table of Contents

4

Introduction

Do you have difficulty dealing with emotional pain?

Do you find yourself making impulsive and self-destructive decisions on a regular basis?

If this is the case, you may be experiencing the signs and symptoms of a wounded inner child.

Now more than ever, many people are suffering from severe emotional pain and are unable to acknowledge what their inner child is trying to tell them about themselves. They are completely unaware of the amount of unresolved emotional pain they are carrying around with them. Likewise, they are perplexed as to why they are constantly depressed, anxious, victimized, and disappointed. They struggle to determine why they continue to make the same self-destructive impulsive decisions.

These patterns are frequently the result of the individual's wounded inner child, which carries a false story that has been repeated over and over since childhood. Symptoms from childhood experiences of abuse, neglect, or trauma manifest themselves as explosive anger, isolation, poor relationship choices, negative self-talk, severe anxiety and people pleasing.

Inner Child Healing will teach you how to get to the root of what's making you uncomfortable and to discover the true essence of who you really are. You will learn effective strategies to ultimately heal your wounded inner child.

With the help of this book, you will learn how to develop a self-nurturing strategy and how to gain a better understanding of your relationships, codependency patterns, and triggering events.

Who Created This Book?

My name is Damian Blair. During my tenure as therapist, I have seen many clients struggle through this unresolved pain, stuck in a pattern of making the same bad impulsive decisions over and over again. I wrote "Inner Child Healing" to allow others to set themselves free by getting to the root of their discomfort. My hope is that after reading this guide you will have the knowledge you need to move forward in confidence.

How Is This Book Structured?

There are ten chapters in this book. In the first chapter, you'll discover what your inner child is and why connecting with them is beneficial. To help you better understand your inner child, I'll go over the many archetypes and characteristics so can you select the one that most closely matches your personality.

In the second chapter, we'll look at how abandonment anxieties manifest in adults and how they relate to the child within. You'll also discover how alcoholic parenting affects our inner child, and how trauma can cause us to suffer emotional losses that are "under-the-surface".

After that, you'll be introduced to critical techniques for reclaiming your inner child and healing your past traumas. As we move into chapter three, you'll discover how to communicate effectively with your inner child using exercises such as letter writing, affirmations, journaling, and more.

Getting in touch with your shadow self is something we'll cover in depth in chapter four. For mending your inner child, this section will teach you to embrace your dark side or hidden personality traits and how self-awareness of them can lead to healing.

In the fifth chapter, you'll discover how to establish personal boundaries. Establishing limits is critical, and this chapter will show you how to do so step-by-by-step while also setting caring intentions for yourself.

In chapter six, we'll talk about how your inner child affects your most intimate connections. If you address your wounded inner child, it can become a hindrance and catalyst for conflict in your relationships. You'll discover ways to jump-start the healing process and build stronger bonds with others.

Your inner child also has an impact on your work, as you'll discover in chapter seven. When you have a wounded inner child, you develop personality traits that are unhelpful and might lead to difficulties in your career. You'll learn how to control these reactions and develop into a more well-rounded and better performing professional as a result.

As you progress through chapter eight, you'll learn how parenting and your inner child influence your financial outlook and behavior. You'll learn how to develop new, more positive attitudes that will assist you in overcoming bad financial habits.

As you progress through chapter nine, you will learn the value of journaling your inner child and receive the most useful writing prompts for enhancing communication and healing.

This book concludes with an easy-to-follow overview of the inner child work that has been described and a breakdown of further activities that can be done to restore your injured inner child.

Having learned the fundamentals of this book, you're ready to begin. At first, what you're about to learn may seem difficult, but it's well worth the effort in the long term.

The next chapter will introduce you to your inner child and the importance of healing any wounds you may have.

Ready? Let's get started!

Chapter 1. What Is Your Inner Child?

Each of us has an inner child, a younger version of ourselves who carries our past experiences, thoughts, and convictions in his or her memory. An important element of our lives is learning how to care for ourselves and live in relationship to others. This is what our childhood signifies in our minds.

Depending on how you were looked after, your inner child can have different levels of unsatisfied needs or lack of self-confidence. Our inner child can unconsciously ruin our life and relationships if we don't complete the therapeutic work to better understand and address these demands.

Perhaps you can relate to some of the following situations:

- You're overworked and feel like everyone wants the world from you. Frustrated, you believe your only option is to go at it alone. When someone offers you help or notices that you are struggling, you refuse. Even though you want to accept the help you've been hoping for, you dig in your heels and say, "too little, too late."

- Your partner is irritated by something you do or do not do, such as how you dry the dishes. It could be anything minor. Although they express it lovingly and in the form of a plea, you can only help but feel strongly criticized. Deep down, you know your partner doesn't intentionally want to attack, but you still feel judged, fatigued and think "I'm never going to be good enough" and shut down.

- While you're waiting for a friend, they text to say they're running late. At first, it doesn't appear to be an issue. Nevertheless, as the minutes tick by, you begin to feel ignored and undervalued, along with increased guilt at being left all alone. The truth is that this friend has a history of showing up late, and while part of you thinks that it's not about them, another side of you believes they don't care, leaving you wondering, "Why am I even here?"

Most of us are aware that our early years have an impact on who we are today, but many of us find it difficult to realize the specific wounds that our inner child may have, especially if we had overbearing parents as children. The more we can move away from the internal stories and go deeper into the details of what our family was like during childhood, we can start seeing what was provided and what could have been lacking.

Being an adult does have its advantages. You can cook anything you want, spend your money as you want, and you no longer need to ask your parents for permission. But, every now and then, something unexpected happens. If a coworker says something hurtful or if you have an argument with your spouse, you may feel as if you're six years old all over again. You may be experiencing "inner child" behavior when this occurs.

The psychological idea of "inner child" refers to the infantile side of your subconscious. It has been discovered that this aspect of the human psyche can be found in all of us, and it influences our daily decisions and actions, either negatively or positively. Psychiatrist Carl Jung is widely believed to have coined the phrase. Inner child is the part of ourselves that is forgiving, free-spirited, and experiences life as if it were a child. But, just as it contains the positive aspects of childhood, such as happiness, purity and imagination, it also contains the scars of our past.

Physical or mental abuse, bullying, or growing up in a shattered household, for example, can cause these wounds. But if this occurred, some may find that the agony persists for the rest of their lives, reappearing at the most inconvenient moments. When it comes to these setbacks, "reparenting" your inner child can be a lifesaver. Returning to past events might help us understand some of the causes for our current anxieties, phobias, and behavioral patterns. True healing can only begin when we start to recognize and understand them for what they truly are.

Your inner child is a tool for recalling memories and sensations from the past, not an entity in and of itself; it is ultimately responsible for molding you into the person you are now.

Our inner child is a self-sufficient and concealed form that exists deep within us. When given expression, it undergoes transformation. A common misconception is that the term "inner child" describes a part of your brain that harbors childhood fantasies. In reality, the inner child is the childlike aspect of your unconscious mind that you can observe and experience. With both positive and negative characteristics, it depicts the child we once were.

The inner child is employed as a conceptual framework to examine our developmental issues and the development of our personalities. Every one of us have the power to meet our unmet needs and express suppressed childhood emotions. We also possess the ability to retain our young innocence, experience natural enthusiasm, and exhibit our creative abilities.

When we think of "repressed feelings," everything that you have been taught that you are not permitted to feel when you wish to embrace affection is included. As a result, the inner child within you continues to hold on to the sadness, anger, and trauma that arose from being rejected by your parents.

It is in this sense that the inner child continues to exist within us, becoming a part of our awareness through the images that it makes for us. The result is that our interactions with everyone else are influenced.

The Benefits of Inner Child Connection

How might working with our inner child serve us as adults? It may seem contradictory to delve into the past when coping with current concerns. However, "reparenting" your inner child can benefit you in the following ways:

- You can discover and heal any repressed emotions you may have had as a child.
- You are able to determine the source of any phobias or unhelpful patterns.
- You can increase your self-esteem and compassion for yourself.
- You are able to make self-care a part of your daily routine.
- You can unleash your playful, creative, and fun side.

It's important to note that not all therapists place a high value on the past or engage with the inner child. If you're doing cognitive behavioral therapy, then the psychologist will look at your present ideas, behaviors, and emotions and explain how they're all interconnected with one another. This is especially true if your problems are new, like personal grief where your symptoms only recently manifested.

Many people, on the other hand, realize that their difficulties are tied to their early childhood experiences, which is especially true if they have a long-standing problem that they haven't been able to manage on their own. It is at this point that working with your inner child is essential.

So how do you know if inner child work is right for you?

In the end, it all comes down to what's bothering you, your symptoms, and your long-term objectives. Many troubles can ultimately be resolved by healing your inner child. If your upbringing was traumatic, you're prone to toxic relationships, or you're unable to connect with others on an emotional level, you may benefit greatly from it.

Let's say you're prone to being in codependent relationships because of your personality. The interpersonal dynamic is unbalanced since one person frequently gives while the other takes. Overprotective or under protective parents are frequently to blame for the emergence of codependency. Even if your parents were well-intentioned, you may have been held back by their over protectiveness. Your inability to identify and communicate your needs as an adult may be the outcome of this early experience.

You're more likely to fall into co-dependent relationships if you don't trust your own judgment and require a lot of reassurance. On the other hand, if your parents were overprotective, you might have been expected to just "get on with it" and take care of yourself. A lack of a safety net can cause you to feel alienated and alone. Codependent relationships may appeal to you because you want to feel needed.

Keeping this in mind, looking into your past may be able to help you identify the source of your codependency, while the reparenting of your inner child can help end its cycle.

Archetypes of the Inner Child

Inner child archetypes are classified into six types. Each one has positive and negative characteristics that emerge throughout our lifetime. There is a child archetype in all of us at some point, but our actual inner child is the archetype that most often resonates with you personally.

Orphan Child

The orphan child archetype, also known as the abandoned child, manifests itself as a child who is self-sufficient throughout their lives. The orphan child likes to learn things on their own, shun groups, and overcome their concerns because they have a history of feeling lonely, emotionally abandoned, or actually orphaned.

In a negative context, this child archetype may isolate oneself and refuse to allow loved ones into their lives to their disadvantage. Postpartum depression sufferers may overcompensate by searching out surrogate families on a regular basis to replace the emotional emptiness.

Wounded Child

The archetype of the wounded child is linked to memories of an abusive or difficult upbringing in one's youth. Throughout their lives, they may have been subjected to a tremendous amount of physical and emotional abuse, typically by multiple people. When this archetype is balanced and embraced, they have the potential to awaken the world to a deep compassion for individuals who are victims of violent relationships. Their perspective switches to one of forgiveness and empathy as they dedicate themselves to helping other traumatized victims heal.

If perceived in a bad light, this child archetype may become locked in an abusive pattern of behavior with lovers, coworkers, and friends. They become accustomed to playing the victim and place the blame for all of their problems squarely on the shoulders of their dysfunctional upbringing.

The Eternal Child

The archetype of the eternal child is perpetually young. This archetype, who exhibits classic childlike characteristics, is adamant about not growing up and is constantly on the lookout for fun and playful ways to approach life. This personality type, who in some ways resembles Peter Pan, is motivated to stay young in mind, body, and spirit, and urges others to do the same.

The implication is that this child will become reckless and unreliable, rendering him or her incapable of carrying out adult obligations. They may have difficulty accepting the personal boundaries of others and may become overly reliant on their loved ones to look after them in their old age.

The Magical Child

We all have a magical child inside of us when we're young, the part that's enchanted and sees the world as limitless. They are frequently carefree, looking for the wonder and beauty in all things, and they have a strong belief that they can do anything they set their minds to. They are dreamers in every sense of the word.

In contrast, if the magical child archetype is not kept in balance, they can develop into a pessimistic and depressed person. There is a crushing effect on their beliefs, and they begin to be cynical about things that they once spent hours fantasizing about. Another risk is that they will lose touch with reality if they immerse themselves in a fantasy world through the usage of role-playing games, fiction literature, or films, while also taking little initiative in their own life.

Divine Child

The Divine Child archetype is connected with attributes such as innocence, purity, and a Godlike quality that is impossible to attain. In addition to having a strong belief in the prospect of redemption, they are typically intensely spiritually linked. If you look closely, this child archetype can appear mystical and surreal. Few people choose this archetype for themselves because they do not believe they possess the necessary abilities. However, it's possible that the divine child is dormant inside of you, just waiting for the ideal circumstances to emerge so you can reach your full capabilities.

Its negative characteristics may be more familiar to you than its more noticeable ones. This archetype is frequently overwhelmed by negative energies and believes that they are powerless to defend themselves. When confronted with evil, they may become easily enraged and unable to control their emotions, causing them to lose control and become fearful of themselves.

The Nature Child

Since they were young, the nature child archetypes have had a profound emotional attachment to plants, animals, and the natural world around them. Animal companionship makes them happier, and they may be able to speak with them as well as the rest of nature. It is common for this archetype to dream about their animal spirit guardians.

The nature child's darker side manifests itself in physical aggression toward those around them. They have the potential to turn violent toward animals, plants, and even humans. Even though they have a strong bond with nature, they can use it as a punishment rather than a source of delight.

Everyone can relate to one or more of these archetypes at some point in their lives; but, one specifically will continually reveal itself to you over time. As you learn to recognize your inner child's strengths and weaknesses, and as you observe how this inner child manifests itself in your life, you will begin to bring your child archetype back into balance and to recognize its playful positivity once more.

Trauma And The Inner Child

How can you tell if a traumatic event from your past is still affecting you today? Is it linked to your inner child in any way?

Here are several indications that you may be dealing with a wounded inner child:

- You have a deep-seated sense that something is wrong with you.
- When you step outside of your comfort zone, you may experience anxiety.
- You have a strong desire to please others.
- You feel that a strong sense of your own identity is absent from your life.
- You actively seek out situations in which you are at odds with the people around you.
- You have a hard time letting go of things, feelings, and people you care about.
- You may be feeling insufficient in your gender role.
- You are continually berating yourself for your perceived inferiority and incompetence.
- You're hard on yourself, unyielding, and a stickler for perfection.
- You have a difficult time making commitments and placing your trust in others.
- You suffer from severe abandonment concerns and would cling to relationships, even if they were harmful to your health.

To be honest, we all have traumas from our pasts that need to be addressed, no matter how minor or inconsequential our role in society may be. The inner child mirrors the child we once were. It is the script we learned at an early age and how to deal with emotions, issues and relationships.

We all have an inner child, and as we get older, that part of us comes out when confronted with a new situation or circumstance. This means that if your eight-year-old self was hurt or traumatized, even if you're an adult now, it's your eight-year-old self who is reacting to similar difficulties in your life since the wound hasn't healed.

When we don't identify or heal those scars, we typically answer from the wounded spot. That is to say, rather than responding to the circumstance as an adult, we respond from a traumatized state.

It also allows us to see our early trauma more objectively when we engage in inner child work. In retrospect, we tend to see things from an adult perspective rather than from the perspective of a child when reliving our childhood experiences. However, while we now realize that the incident may not have been a "big deal," our pain at the time was real. Learning to connect with the inner child, validating the grief and healing without judgment helps us respond better to our current emotions and needs.

The Process of Inner Child Work

Inner child work, also known as inner child healing, is a technique for addressing the needs we didn't have met as children and mending the attachment scars we've formed as a result of that neglect. Every one of us has a younger version of ourselves that was "never exactly loved in the proper manner or required as a child," according to clinical psychologist Trish Phillips.

The process of inner child work, as with any sort of inner work, entails establishing a space where your subconscious can take the reins. Investigating our true emotions and psyche that may have been rejected and judged as "wrong" or "too much" by others is what is referred to as "inner work." The act of taking the time to go within begins the process of removing our everyday coping methods (such as avoiding our feelings or feeling nothing at all) and allowing our subconscious to be fully accepted and integrated into the conscious.

With maturity comes the opportunity to repair the wounds of our wounded inner child and to create the supportive, nurturing environments that our younger selves wished they had.

The Importance of Inner Child Healing

The wounds from our childhood follow us into adulthood. They might be basic or complex trauma, ranging from emotional neglect to physical violence. According to Phillips, many people believe they are alone in their hurt, and as a result, they choose to conceal the trauma because they believe that is "what other grown-ups do."

That is why inner child healing is so crucial. It ultimately serves two purposes: to provide a constant reminder that we are right and to help us overcome the shame that exists with merely being aware of the sensations we are having.

Through the healing of our inner child, we can begin to build the sense of protection and stability that our younger selves have always craved and deserved. The beneficial characteristics of our inner child are given more opportunity to shine as a result. We discover our innate abilities, our inner curiosity, and our unlimited capacity for love. We are transformed.

Chapter 2. The Adult Who Never Grew Up

We were all once children, and we all have a part of ourselves that is still a child. However, the majority of adults are completely unaware of this. This lack of connection to our inner child is the root of many behavioral, emotional, and interpersonal issues we face today.

As it turns out, the vast majority of so-called adults aren't actually adults at all. Even though we are getting older, this is not adulthood from a psychological standpoint. Being a true adult is dependent on one's ability to recognize, embrace, and accept responsibility for one's own inner child. Unfortunately, this never happens to many adults. Instead, their parents, teachers, and other adults have denied or rejected their inner child. Society ultimately expects us to "grow up" and put our adolescent ways behind us.

In reality, these so-called "adults" are unintentionally being influenced or dominated by their unconscious inner child on a continuous basis. Rather than an adult self-controlling their actions, many people are guided by an emotionally wounded inner child. A five-year-old running around in a forty-year-body old's body is a sight to behold. It is a hurt, angry, and terrified little boy or girl who is in charge, making decisions for himself or herself-- a boy or a girl who has been sent out into the world to carry out the duties of a man or a woman. They are a child attempting to engage in mature social interactions.

Without a doubt, a child is unable to live a self-sufficient life.

Nonetheless, if we have a wounded inner child, we start to wonder why our relationships are failing us. We're not sure why we're feeling so worried, fearful or insecure. After all, how else would any child feel if they were forced to fend for themselves in what appears to be an adult environment? What would happen if you didn't have sufficient parental protection, structure, or support?

This is the perplexing condition of affairs that is encountered so regularly among those seeking therapy. It is not a dissociative identity disorder but rather a far more widespread, persistent, and insidious type of dissociation that has become prevalent. Nevertheless, if we can see the problem for what it is, we may begin to deal with it by making the decision to become psychological adults rather than just chronological adults.

So how do we begin to address this?

To begin, one must become conscious of one's own inner child and learn to accept it. A person's inner child might take control of their personality and thwart their will just by remaining hidden. Taking our inner child seriously and actively speaking with that young boy or girl within teaches us to listen and understand what he or she needs from us at this moment, rather than dismissing them. We still have the same primordial needs as we did when we were children, including love, acceptance, protection, nurturing, and understanding. These desires, which are frequently unfulfilled, are the same today as they were then. As pseudo-adults, we make unsuccessful attempts to coerce others into fulfilling our infantile wants on behalf of ourselves. This, however, is doomed to failure. We must confront what we did not get adequately from our parents as children in the past, no matter how painful the experience may be in this present moment.

Trauma and disappointment experienced in the past cannot be changed and must be acknowledged. Being an adult necessitates swallowing the "bitter pill" because, for the vast majority of us, our imperfect parents or caregivers either failed to provide certain developmental necessities or did so inadvertently. That isn't going to change, no matter how intelligent or loving we become. It is impossible to undo what has been done. As adults, we shouldn't expect people to fulfill all of our unmet childhood demands. They are simply unable to. Acknowledging and accepting one's painful past while also gaining responsibility for taking care of one's inner child's needs is required for authentic maturity.

When it comes to psychotherapy, a reconciliation between the inner child and the mature adult can be achieved through the establishment and maintenance of an ongoing dialogue between the two. It is possible to establish a new, cooperative, symbiotic relationship in which the contradictory demands of the adult self and the inner child can be met.

The Inner Child & Abandonment Fears

Fear of abandonment is a multifaceted issue that can have its roots in a range of life events, such as loss or trauma. This phobia has been examined from a number of angles. This fear can be explained by a variety of factors, including a child experiencing difficulties with cognitive or emotional development, problems in a previous relationship, or other negative social or life situations.

Being abandoned is one of the most widespread and destructive emotions, despite the fact that it is not an acknowledged phobia. People who are afraid of abandonment may engage in actions and patterns of thinking that have an impact on their personal relationships and mental health.

The following instances are the most common ways in which abandonment fears can have a negative impact on your relationships with the people who are important to you.

When your loved ones don't get in touch with you on a regular basis, you become concerned.

You're the type of person that begins texting your significant other the moment they fail to check in with you. It's impossible not to drive them insane and cause terror the moment they're too quiet, believing that something terrible has happened to them. Perhaps something horrific occurred during your childhood, which makes it clear why you are feeling this way.

When you become too close to someone, you withdraw from the relationship.

Your abandonment concerns will come to the surface the moment you become too close to someone you care about. You have a deep-seated dread that your partner may abandon you. As a result, you are the first to go.

You come up with the most ludicrous reason to end your relationship with them, despite the fact that you are still passionately in love with them. Everything seems to make no sense — but keep in mind that you're dealing with an inner child here. They do not act logically; instead, they act on emotion.

You develop a desire to satisfy others.

Do you find yourself saying yes when you actually want to say no all the time? Due to your constant efforts to satisfy others, you are the type of person who everyone enjoys having around them. To make matters worse, you're pleasing everyone except yourself.

To protect yourself from being abandoned, you believe that making everyone happy will ensure that they will never abandon your side of the family. This, however, will not persist. Because no one can please everyone all of the time, and if you try, you will burn yourself out sooner or later. The reality is that no matter how good you are to somebody, they may still decide to leave you. As a result, you should put yourself first and foremost in your priorities.

In relationships, you give far too much of yourself.

When it comes to your interpersonal interactions, you are frequently the giver. It is possible to become codependent with someone and to give far more than you receive in return. You are the partner that is constantly showering your loved one with extravagant gifts. It's almost as though you believe you must purchase someone's affection. You hurry over to assist them with everything they require, frequently forgetting your own needs in the process. Because you have no boundaries, opportunists will take advantage of you. You do this because, deep down, the child in you feels that if you provide enough for them, your spouse will never want to leave you.

You have problems placing your faith in others.

No matter how well things are going in your relationship, you are always on the lookout for when the other shoe is going to fall. You have a hard time believing that the person you love would stay by your side this time, and that you could finally be in a mutually loving relationship with them.

You will be insecure, you will question them if they are out for an extended period of time, and you will not believe what they are telling you. This is your inner child reacting because you were taught not to be trusting as a result of early trauma.

You are under the impression that you are not good enough.

If your parent abandoned you, it's possible that you absorbed the experience, feeling it was entirely your responsibility. It was because you were unlovable that they decided to leave you. You go through life prepared to fail, not simply in relationships but in general.

In approaching a relationship with a partner with this perspective, you are setting the relationship up for failure from the get-go. Your deepest secret is that you believe you are unworthy of being with the person you are now with, and you expect them to feel the same way about you because you do not value yourself. You treat them as if they are superior to you, and you as if you are inferior to them.

If you were mistreated as a child, it's possible that you'll accept this as normal in a relationship when it isn't in reality.

You have innate beliefs that will have a negative impact on your life.

If you grew up in a family that believed that working a 9–5 job was the only way to achieve success, you may grow up feeling that this is the only way to work as an adult. If you are more suited to more creative and enjoyable work that does not necessitate standard working hours, it may hinder your advancement in your profession.

If you were raised with the belief that wealth is a bad thing, you may unconsciously avoid acquiring it, which will have a detrimental impact on your financial situation later in life.

If you were taught as a child that you were the "slow one," you will grow up feeling that you are not intelligent. This is something your inner child will always believe. It keeps you from obtaining a higher education because you believe you are not intelligent enough to do so which could have long-term consequences for your professional life.

Likewise, if you were told as a child that you were not attractive, you will grow up believing that you are not attractive enough to attract the person you desire, and this will ruin your future romantic relationships.

Alcoholic Parenting & The Adult Child

When one or both parents are alcoholics, it can make life for a child feel quite unpredictable. As a result of the toll alcoholism takes on the family, children of alcoholics are more likely to experience emotional or behavioral problems throughout their lives, especially as they get older. Furthermore, if a child's emotional requirements aren't satisfied throughout critical developmental years, he or she may grow up unsure of how to meet those needs as an adult. Consequently, children who have grown up around alcoholics are more likely to exhibit specific features and personality traits as adults, which can have an impact on their social interactions, self-perception, and emotional and behavioral state. Recognizing these personality and character qualities might therefore assist an adult child of an alcoholic move ahead, possibly through support groups, to prevent these traits from destroying a stable and healthy lifestyle.

One of the most difficult challenges for adult children to deal with is the fact that part, if not the majority, of their grieving stems from a period in their childhood. Many of them believe they are too old to express the amount of pain that they are genuinely experiencing. Possibly, some of them have more positive relationships with their sober parents. They don't want to put their relationship in danger by releasing their sorrow right now, but it still has to be felt and processed because they are still carrying it and possibly living it out. As a result, an adult child may find themselves in a difficult situation. It is possible that the child within is still in agony even if they have finally gotten what they've always wanted—a sober parent and a comfortable relationship with them—and that they will continue to cry and become furious.

It is likely that the adult child is in love with their now-sober parent, and that the parent wishes to forget about all of those horrible years, or at least the half of them that they don't remember. They want to make amends and get it over with as soon as possible. It is not finished for the adult child, however, and they are now left with the difficult chore of loving their sober parent while also needing to confront the parent with whom they grew up in an abusive relationship. They must grieve for that parent, get angry at them, and ultimately confront them with their wrongdoing. But they're reluctant to do so since they've finally gotten what they've always wanted: a sober parental figure. And, they too, don't want to be the ones to cause a commotion.

For the ordinary adult child, it will take time before they can go on. In order for these adult children to genuinely communicate from the perspective of their inner child to the parent they had at the time, it is necessary that they do so. This is made much more efficient, clear, and healing through the use of role play.

The ability to let the child or injured part of themselves to communicate with their adult self is something I educate clients to do before blazing their sentiments into the world and being disappointed that no one listens or cares. It is our responsibility as grownups to hear ourselves, to be our own good parents, and to pay attention to everything that the many aspects of ourselves try to tell us.

When we are able to communicate in this manner, we have a decent chance of being understood. When we can listen while someone else tries to do the same with us, we lay the groundwork for closeness and success in our relationships, whether they are with friends or colleagues at work. We'll have our moments of rage, our tears, our frustrations, and meltdowns, but they must be brief. This is important. Forgiveness and understanding must be restored as quickly as possible.

It's a shame that we avoid grief because, in all honesty, it's the quickest way to go over whatever is preventing us from experiencing joy. Furthermore, if you truly allow yourself to feel pain, you will cry, become angry, and feel thrown around, but you will also feel liberated and soothed. And all of this manifests itself in waves. If you don't resist it or become stuck in it, you'll see fantastic results.

Disenfranchised Losses

Death, for example, is an unmistakable loss. Society regards it as significant, and we have established ceremonies to help cope. When grieving, we are confident in our ability to ask for help, and it is often given to us without our having to ask. However, the types of losses that accompany relational trauma and addiction are not always acknowledged and grieved. As a result, they frequently continue to be classified as "disenfranchised."

Losses resulting from disenfranchisement can be difficult to see and understand. It is as if they have been split out of consciousness and are often unnoticed or misinterpreted by others, as well as ourselves. In some circumstances, it's difficult to determine who or what has been lost, or even if a loss has occurred.

The reality is that not only do these losses exist, but their failure to be acknowledged or grieved can create roadblocks in our journey of grieving and healing. These kinds of tragedies necessitate our compassion and attention. People who experience bereavement due to various kinds of losses may undergo internal change, which may then manifest externally as well.

Disenfranchised losses can include any of the following:

- Trauma-induced disconnection from one's self
- If you're an addict, you've lost a functional part of your life
- The absence of a sober parent or of a carefree period of childhood.
- The loss of a functional family
- Miscarriage, infertility or disabling health conditions
- Relocating to a new residence
- Losing one's work or retiring
- Mental illness or cognitive deficit

Understanding and processing our losses can be the catalyst for moving on and growing, as well as for releasing our inner child from the shadows. When we deal with a loss, it might evoke memories or bring up other losses, which adds to the difficulty of grieving. This is one of the factors that contribute to the difficulty of mourning.

Putting ourselves into a character or a series of roles in a psychodrama allows us to put the actual loss we're experiencing into perspective. An empty chair can signify a portion of one's self, a period of one's life, a person, or even a substance in some instances. As we converse with it, we can have a spontaneous and honest exchange that helps us connect with our feelings or parts of ourselves that we have lost contact with.

Journaling or letter writing are other effective methods of releasing and processing emotions such as sadness, anger, and loss. Simply pour your sentiments onto the paper and allow them to flow. Losing a sense of self or of someone significant, losing a link to the sober parent, losing a sense of a time in one's life, losing a sense of familial function is just as important as mourning the loss of a life.

Individuals who are grieving a disenfranchised loss sometimes feel alone in their feelings, but being in a small group of people, can provide a sense of permission and freedom in facing them.

Chapter 3. Reparenting: Inner Child Work

Inner child work is intended to help you free the shame that has bound you– to establish a connection and relationship with your inner child– as well as to allow your true self to emerge from the shadows into light. It is possible to have a conscious relationship with yourself and make choices— choices that have been thought through and are not made on the spur of the moment.

It is freeing and illuminating to come to terms with one's own identity for the very first time. Remove the survival suit and you will be able to express yourself more authentically. It is being real that allows you to be able to embrace your own being. When self-doubt and poor self-esteem are conquered, they are replaced by confidence and self-worth. There is a feeling of completeness. It is possible to make better decisions when you have a healthy relationship with yourself.

Owning your shadow side and loving yourself are all important steps. A mindful interaction with someone is encouraged, whether with your partner, spouse, children, family, or other acquaintances.

It's true that working with one's inner child can be challenging, but it's nothing compared to the years of pain and suffering one has had to undergo before deciding to engage in the process. The pain during recovery is short-lived because the individual's repressed sentiments are brought to the top of his or her conscious mind throughout the procedure. When relief finally arrives, it is accompanied by new understanding, not only on a cognitive level, but also on an experiential level that is more closely associated with the healing process.

Reparenting the Inner Child

You are every age you have ever been, which means that at any given time, you are carrying the wisdom of your oldest self as well as the naivety of your youngest self. In many cases, persons who were subjected to abuse or neglect as children have scars that have been buried deep within their psyche as they have grown older. Individuals who have not experienced major trauma may nevertheless have terrible experiences or things said to them that have stayed with them throughout their lives.

In order to prevent your inner child from becoming stuck and negatively damaging your present-day emotions and experiences, it is critical to nurture and provide healing to this part of yourself. The brain is particularly receptive at a young age, up until the age of roughly four years. This means that our emotional routines and the information we employ in the future will be heavily influenced by our experiences up to that time. Our brains evolved a unique set of survival mechanisms as a result of the roles we were taught to play as children (verbally or nonverbally).

We honed these techniques by seeing how others in our lives dealt with their emotions, notably sadness and indignation, and learning from their examples. When you make future decisions, your unconscious mind will be guided by this script. There is no other way to look at the narrative than to nurture and re-parent your inner child.

Are you unsure of where to begin? It's easy to be intimidated by the prospect of doing inner child work. However, the good news is that it is quite similar to self-care. To put it another way, inner child work is about learning to be your own parent. It's about being kind to yourself, being aware of your thoughts, feelings, and needs, and healing whatever pain you may have experienced as a child.

So, what is the best way to go about accomplishing this?

First and first, you must acknowledge the existence of your inner child in order to nurture and heal them. It is critical that your inner child understands that they have the ability to break out from the pattern of the past—but this can only happen if safety has been established.

The Power of Inner Child Work

The process by which you deal with your inner child will decide how things turn out. Instead of seeing your inner child as a threat, look at it as an ally. You've dealt with the negative voice in your head for as long as you've had it. To receive the affection you never received as a child, you must being the process of reaching out and being heard.

Your inner work begins with re-parenting yourself. You must grow into the caring adult you felt you lacked as a child. It's difficult for me to accept this. However, you are solely responsible for your emotions. You must give yourself the love you can only give to yourself.

It's important, however, to know the risks before you start. The first step in working with your inner child is likely to make you feel quite emotional. It may be difficult to discover your inner child. If you've experienced mild to severe physical abuse, you may require guidance from a third party. Don't be deterred, though. Give them a shot. You have nothing to lose by giving it a try. These self-healing exercises can be life-changing. Be aware of your restrictions, however. They're designed such that you can engage with them most successfully based on how you interacted with them in the past.

The only way positive things can happen is if you accept your inner child's struggle. Your traumas have been suppressed for a long time, which may explain why you feel out of sorts. The most important thing to focus on is keeping an eye out for anything unusual. Pay close attention to how you react and what triggers that reaction. Patterns in your behavior are what you're after. You can begin tracing your actions back to the source of the problem once you've determined how you're behaving right now.

Mirror Gazing Technique

Reconnecting with your inner child can be as simple as using the mirror gazing technique, commonly known as "mirror work."

Make sure you have some privacy before attempting this technique in the presence of others. A neutral state of mind is required, so don't try this if you're depressed or under stress.

First, find a mirror, put your palm on your heart, and look at yourself with compassion.

Do this for five minutes.

At first, thoughts and even emotions will bubble to the surface. Allow them to go unnoticed and don't get emotionally invested with them. Observe them in the same way you would a cloud in the sky. Also, keep in mind that it's appropriate to isolate yourself, especially if you're experiencing sadness.

Next, when you're ready, channel your inner child. Speaking out or talking silently in your head both work. When you see your inner child appearing in your eyes, say something loving and nice to this vulnerable aspect of you. You may say something like, "I see you," "I'm proud of you," or "I believe you're brave and powerful," or anything else that comes to mind. Pay attention to your internal reactions. Most importantly, use this as a chance to cultivate self-compassion and love, especially in the face of tough or powerful emotions.

In order to complete this exercise, tell your inner child whatever is currently on your mind and heart.

Writing A Letter To Your Inner Child

This activity requires you to write a letter to a younger version of yourself. With this exercise you will be able to:

- Validate your childhood trauma, pain or disappointment
- Eliminate any feelings of blame or shame for situations over which you had no control
- Retrospectively offer compassion to your childhood self that was missing at the time
- Begin to heal historic wounds

For this activity, you will write about the problems you had as a child and the impact they had on your life. You will encourage and console the inner child by reassuring them that it is acceptable to grieve and then asking them to let go of the pain in order to make place for a better future.

You will need a pencil, paper and candle for this exercise.

First, find a quiet spot to sit and relax. You can either practice this in the great outdoors or in a peaceful corner of your house. If it helps, light a candle before you begin.

It is best to have a specific recollection or occurrence in mind before you begin this activity (for example: a specific memory of being bullied in high school).

If you're not sure when the specific moment is, but you're conscious that you need to heal something, take a deep breath and see what age comes up for you. If you're like most people, this will come to you as some sort of image. Don't make any assumptions about it, and just go with the flow.

Begin your letters with the salutation "Dear Little [Your Name]" to establish an adult point of view.

Once you've done that, write a letter to your inner child in which you express your love for him or her, assure them that it's okay for them to share their hurt feelings or memories with you, and let them know you're here to listen to all they have to say.

Continue with your writing until all of the advice to your young self has been expressed. Set your pencil down when you feel you have finished speaking to them.

Writing To Your Adult Self

You can learn a lot about yourself if you write from the viewpoint of your inner child instead of your adult self. However, it's a good idea to start with the previous letter, as it may take some practice to write from your own inner child.

If you feel ready to being communicating in this manner, write Dear Adult [Your Name] on a different sheet of paper. Allow yourself to write freely to your adult self from the viewpoint of your inner child. Allow them to say what they need to say without interfering or making judgments about what is said. Allow them to speak. You might get the impression that they're depressed from their words. They could also be enraged. Allow them the opportunity to express themselves after such a long period of silence.

If you are having issues channeling your inner child, use your opposite hand to write the letter. This can help people who are having problems using their imagination to get out of their heads.

Finally, take a moment to read both of these letters aloud to yourself once your inner child has finished speaking. When we use our voices and hear with our ears what we're healing from, it's quite powerful and can assist us in developing self-compassion. Spend some time contemplating the words that have been written to you.

You might also write back and forth between your adult and inner child until you feel understood. Be receptive to your body's message about what you need to hear in your life. Cry if you need to. If you're upset, yell into a pillow or slam your fists into the ground. Do this practice while allowing your emotions to flow.

After you've finished writing, blow out the candle as a sign that you're finished and ready to move on.

You can create a symbolic ritual with these letters once you've finished writing and feel satisfied with the results. Consider offering them to nature to help you move through the healing process:

- Dispose of the letters in a river or burn them (safely)
- Place them in a grave and bury them.

Writing an Unsent Letter To Your Parents

If your parents were a source of stress in your childhood, you might want to consider writing a letter to them. Without consideration for other people's feelings, writing as your childhood self is a healing practice rather than a letter you will send.

The goal of this activity isn't to make things better between you and your parents. The goal is to come to terms with one's innermost thoughts and feelings.

Introduce yourself in your letter with the standard salutation, "Dear Mom and Dad." As you imagine yourself writing directly to them, challenge yourself to share your most intimate truth with them. Don't worry about censoring it. By expressing all of your feelings, including those that are forbidden, you bring them into the open, where you can examine and sift through them, deciding what to keep and what to discard. You have the ability to choose which thoughts are beneficial to you and which ones are damaging.

After you've finished writing your letter, go over it again and ask yourself the following questions: What exactly is lacking? What have I forgotten to include? Is there anything else that needs to be said? What did I take away from this experience?

Once you've finished this task, you might want to write a real letter to your parents. This is okay. You also have the option of doing it that way if you so desire. But first, use this chance to send an unsent letter to yourself in which all of your childhood sorrows can be expressed.

Engage in Carefree Fun

As youngsters, we were frequently given the opportunity to engage in activities solely for recreational purposes—these are the activities that we wanted to do rather than the activities that we had to perform. They are activities that offered us pure joy, rather than activities from which we hoped to make money.

Are there any hobbies or pastimes you've given up because you think they're juvenile or you've "grown out of them?" How many have you given up because you think they're not useful? Now is a good time to give them another shot.

As adults, we are frequently under the impression that we must be serious and mature. However, there is nothing quite as rejuvenating as returning to the hobbies you enjoyed as a child, whether they were skating, arts and crafts, or drama.

Child development is aided by children's participation in play, which serves as a fundamental component of learning and growth. Especially if you weren't given the opportunity to engage with your friends, this could be a crucial step towards reconnecting with your inner child. Growing older, we reprioritize play, often infantilizing it by claiming that it is too juvenile for grown adults to partake in. Despite the fact that this is completely false, it is true that play has the ability to heal.

Were there ever toys or games you yearned for as a kid but were denied access to? A trampoline, an easy bake oven, or a trip to an amusement park are all possibilities. If it's possible, make an investment in that experience for yourself as an adult. Create opportunities that are solely concerned with having a good time.

Consider jumping off the swings at a park, where you could think to yourself, "I'm channeling my inner child." Alternatively, you can get a rush of sheer ecstasy when you go skateboarding or jump into a lake while wearing your clothing. Although it may appear ridiculous, there is a reason why engaging in childlike pastimes can be so liberating.

Affirmations For Your Inner Child

Positive self-talk, such as using affirmations, is a great approach to heal your emotional wounds. They're a huge step up from just talking to your inner child. They're ultimately empowering. It's also the point at which the real work begins.

Get as specific as possible when it comes to your life goals now. The information from the letter-writing tasks can serve as a guide for your search. Because you're looking for something more complex than a standard piece of dialogue, your writings will be a great source of reference. Changing the negative thought processes that are holding you back will help you have a better relationship with yourself going forward. You may do this by rewiring your subconscious mind. The initial words of every declaration should be, 'I am.' Making this connection with your heart area makes it much easier to bring about the changes you desire.

Here are some statements to help you get started:

- I feel more in touch with my inner child than I have in a long time.
- I am grateful that my inner child is here.
- With my inner child, I feel at ease.
- My inner child is worthy of love as they are
- My inner child deserves to have the space and freedom to do what they love

Go Through Old Photographs of Yourself as a Child

Go through your old photo albums to see what you looked like when you were younger. You should keep that picture in your mind because it will help you when you're working with your inner kid. Some people like to keep pictures of themselves as children on their nightstand, in their wallet, or all throughout the house as a way to remember their inner child's existence.

Journaling

Journaling is one of the most effective tools for improving oneself and growing as a person. In reality, all of the methods listed above can be considered a variety of types of journaling. Using inner child journaling prompts can help you get to the bottom of your childhood wounds and work toward healing them. This will be covered in more depth in a separate chapter.

Connecting Through Meditation

Meditation is a powerful tool for exploring the self. Doing an inner journey is a great technique to heal childhood traumas by re-connecting with your inner child. For newcomers, I suggest meditating and visualizing your way through your inner adventures.

First, you must acquire the trust of your inner child by engaging in the previously mentioned activities. This will help you on your inner excursions. Asking your inner child about the events that led to your current trauma is a good first step in developing a close relationship with her.

Using inner child meditation to access your wounded inner child to help you heal yourself is a challenging yet profoundly rewarding technique. According to this belief, you're now in a position to give yourself the compassion you lacked as a youngster. The affection and warmth you were due as a child will never be available to you again, but now is the moment to give it to yourself.

This type of meditation can ultimately help you find and free your inner child.

How to Begin Meditating:

To reconnect with your inner child, practice meditation. Before asking a question, simply take a deep breath, relax, and examine your thoughts. Think about when you first had to deal with a traumatic event and see what comes up for you.

Observe your thoughts as they rise and fall in your mind's atmosphere. The answer may or may not be revealed to you by your inner child. Keep these virtues in mind: patience, love, and acceptance. It's okay if your inner kid refuses to share the answer. There should be a sense of security and comfort for your inner kid.

Try repeating your question a few times if nothing noteworthy comes to mind while you are thinking. A few minutes to an hour or more is possible for this procedure.

A few pointers: You must have prior experience meditating in order to complete this inner child meditation trip successfully. It takes time and effort to become adept at observing your thoughts, so if you aren't used to meditating, you may have difficulty.

Connecting Through Visualization

Visualization is a more active method of connecting with your inner child and past life traumas. If you want to use visualization to connect with your inner child, you'll need a "power spot" or a secure location. In order to achieve this, picture yourself in a beautiful garden, or any other area where you feel secure. You can then allow your inner child to talk with you when you've entered your power place.

Here are the actions you need to take:

- Close your eyes and take a few deep breaths while you relax.
- Visualize yourself descending a stairwell.
- At the bottom of the stairwell, you'll find your power spot or safe haven. You'll get a tremendous sense of security and well-being when you're here.
- Go to your power location and spend some time there. Take everything in. Look, smell, and listen for yourself.
- Then, visualize your younger self having arrived to your power spot, perhaps via a waterfall or a gate.
- Welcome your younger self with a hug.
- Get ready to ask your inner kid questions like, "When was the first time I felt sad or scared?" or something similar. Consider asking the question in terms that children might understand. Keep an eye out for a response.
- Don't forget to thank them, and express how much you appreciate them.
- Then say goodbye.
- Get out of your safe zone and go up the stairwell.
- Regain normal state of mind.

This is a fairly basic process, but it gives you a broad idea of how to go on an inner child journey.

Letter Writing and Sketching

For the following activity, you will need a pencil or crayons and paper.

Close your eyes and relax. Try to imagine a lovely location where you and your inner child can enjoy a trip together. Do what makes you feel safe and comfortable. Trust your instincts.

Open your eyes and use your non-dominant hand to draw a portrait of your inner child. Put yourself in a relaxed and unhurried state by reconnecting with your natural flow within. Using a different piece of paper and your dominant hand (the one you write with most often) take some time to reflect on this process:

- What were your thoughts and feelings while you drew your inner child? Were you frustrated or blocked in any way?
- When you look at the image, how do you feel?
- What origins do you believe you inner child's appearance, such as face expression, location, or clothing, have?
- What age do you think you are in terms of your inner child?

In what ways does your mental image of yourself as a child inform your behavior?

Begin a conversation with your inner child.

As I previously stated, you will now engage in a dialogue with your inner child.

Start by looking at what you've come up with. Use your dominant hand to play the adult. You will then use the non-dominant other hand to reply in the manner of your inner kid.

Once more, follow your gut instincts. Keep in mind that your inner child, like any other child, needs to have faith in you before it can fully develop, so be patient and peaceful when doing these exercises.

Start the conversation by saying to the child that you want to get to know them better so that you can look after them better. Try to learn as much as you can about them by asking for their name and any other personal information they'd want to share with you.

If the dialogue doesn't follow the questions exactly, don't be concerned. Allow yourself to be guided by your gut and go with the flow of events. You can end the talk by asking the child if there is anything else they would like to share with you, and thanking them for speaking out. Tell them you'd like to continue having these discussions.

Reflect back on your inner child's conversation with your dominant hand on a different sheet of paper. This stage is designed to help you become more attuned to the needs of your inner child in the future. Has the conversation revealed anything surprising? Is there a common theme or set of emotions that both the youngster and the adult express? Are there any recollections left?

This approach illuminates our relationship with our inner child in profound ways. With this, we can begin to reconnect with and heal the child inside of us, a part of us that will never grow up, but is yet very real to us.

Connecting with your inner child will give you adult life a whole new depth, revealing the complex personality and the divine, innocent nature of your inner spirit for what they are.

Because the patterns that caused these scars are firmly ingrained in our memory, we can carry them with us everywhere we go and use them to help become a better person every day.

Chapter Summary:

In this chapter, you have learned many ways to begin working on your inner child healing. Here are a few key takeaways:

• **Journal**. A great way to feel emotions and clear your mind is to keep a journal. It's like an act of alchemy to get ideas out of your head and onto paper. Getting started with journaling can be difficult if you aren't sure where to begin. Whatever comes to mind, put it into words. It's impossible to make a mistake. Also, you can use the previously mentioned questions, such as, "What am I feeling?" and "Why am I feeling this?" as prompts to conduct an investigation on paper.

• **Send a letter**. Sending the letter isn't required; however, putting your thoughts down on paper is. Find out why you feel the way you do and communicate your feelings to the person you have in mind. For those who were raised believing that their emotions had no value, this is a great way to prove them wrong. As a symbolic release, consider burning the letter once you've finished it.

• **Meditate**. We may gain insights into why we feel certain ways while meditating. Feeling our emotions can also help us heal on our own accord. Healing occurs in stages, as I've discovered in my own practice. Once I've healed a little, I'll have to come back later to dig a little deeper. However, it's possible for people to have more profound, in-depth encounters on rare occasions. You might want to try meditating on forgiveness. Make a mental image of the inner child and say, "May you be happy, at peace, and free of suffering."

• **Feel**. Feel the intensity of your emotions. Investigate them. Describe them in detail in your writing. Make something creative. Be aware of your true self-worth as a complete being who is worthy of love. Secrets are the lifeblood of the shadow. Bring the parts of yourself you've been hiding out of the spotlight and fill them with self-acceptance. Even if the process is painful, remember that it is normal and that you are not alone.

Chapter 4. Healing Through Shadow Work

Because of our deepest wounds, we believe we're flawed, unlovable, and undeserving of anything good or loving in this world. These scars are frequently created during childhood, but they can also appear later in life. Maybe you've been the victim of bullying or a traumatic life event has left a scar. These wounds can also be cultural. The prevailing social beliefs influence them, such as the connection between money and one's self-worth.

In the absence of treatment, these wounds become infected, forcing us to operate from a position of deficit. Through shadow work, we are able to live from a place of completeness and growth. We stop looking at interactions through the prism of our own past trauma. To a large extent, life revolves around people acting in ways that are predicated on their own lingering wounds, and that's fine.

There's a lot of discussion about love and light in the spiritual world, but before we can experience it, we must first repair the parts of ourselves that we may regard as unattractive or not capable of being loved.

To truly understand ourselves, we must face the darker sides of our personalities, including our rage, resentment, greed, and envy. Disregarding these aspects of our personalities will not make them disappear. Darkness ultimately wields great influence.

Instead of pretending, we become the light by doing shadow work and shedding light on the dark. This practice increases our ability to love ourselves, to have satisfying relationships, and to see the possibilities in our lives.

Doing shadow work is essential for healing and achieving inner peace. In other words, confronting the parts of ourselves that we'd rather ignore or hide.

So, what exactly is this thing we call the shadow?

Carl Jung, the psychoanalyst, coined the term "shadow" to describe our subconscious thoughts and feelings. In order to see your wounded inner child parts and process and heal them, you need to do shadow work, which is simply shining your consciousness' light into your shadow side. To be more accurate, the darkness is caused by your ignorance of what is lurking around the corner. That means you have no idea what's hidden inside—they are things that could trip you up in your day-to-day activities.

A more in-depth look at the shadow's dark characteristics reveals that they are emotional in nature and autonomous in a way with a possessive quality. When we engage in undesirable behaviors, it's not because we have flaws or are deficient in some way; instead, it's because we need help healing our wounded selves.

When we don't take care of our shadow self, it becomes resentful. And the work of healing our wounds provides us with the greatest opportunity to build strength. Our pain is hidden in the shadows, just waiting to be illuminated by our awareness. Workaholism, judgment, and arrogance are all distractions from finding it. It's the mess we're leaving in the basement of our minds because we're too busy to clean it up.

Our shadow is commonly avoided through the following behaviors:

- Overachieving—spiritual bypassing disguised as personal growth. While focusing on the positive aspects of life, we neglect the negative aspects of our lives.
- Overworking in order to keep our minds off of our perceived flaws.
- Chemical addictions, as well as buying things we don't need just to feel and "look" better for a short time.
- Avoidance of true intimacy by hanging out in flimsy relationships.

So how do we actually engage with our shadow?

Compassion for oneself is a good place to start. Avoiding wounds is a human survival mechanism that allows us to continue. You've got a lot on your plate: a career to establish, relationships to tend to, and possibly children to rear. There are good reasons to put off dealing with your issues. If you're a strong willed person, it won't be simple, but the effort will be well worth it.

Keep in mind that no one has ever been in your shoes. Being in the dark brings with it a strong sense of loneliness. However, the number of people who have made it to the other side of the journey is virtually limitless.

For what reasons should we be concerned with the aspects of ourselves that we cannot see?

A person's thoughts, emotions, and behaviors can be adversely affected if their psyche becomes lopsided and the darker aspects of their personality predominate over the lighter aspects.

The Ego's Function

The mind creates what is known as the ego when a person is born. Because information is being processed and stored for later use, the ego's role has changed. When it comes to trauma of any size, the ego doesn't always know how to deal with it fully. As a result, the trauma-related negative emotions will be pushed to the side.

That being said, those strong emotions don't go away by themselves. They can't move forward because they're stuck in the past. This should be done in advance of the emotions showing up at your door to be seen, heard, and processed in the future.

The Work of Self-Healing

An inner healing journey can be beneficial for nearly everyone. One must deliberately go within to see whether there are any lurking shadows that cause negative thoughts, emotions, or behaviors.

If you've been through a lot of trauma in your life, going on an inner-healing journey will be especially beneficial for you. For those who have dealt with trauma in their lives, shadow work with a professional therapist might be beneficial.

Self-directed healing isn't possible for everyone. That's okay. Allow yourself to seek help if you require it.

This type of in-depth emotional work can bring up some very strong emotions, especially if you've been repressing them for a long period of time. Don't try to handle everything on your own; when in doubt, ask for help from a professional.

How to Do Shadow Work

It appears that as our self-awareness increases, we feel and become irritated more because we are more aware of previously unnoticed reactions. This can be a pain, but it's an essential part of the recovery process. Negative feelings open the door to the shadow world. They aid in illuminating the site of the wounds, allowing us to conduct a more thorough examination.

You may, for example, find it irritating when people are good at asking for things. A projection of unmet needs or the secret desire to have the audacity to ask for help could be to blame. You may believe that asking for help is inappropriate or that you do not deserve it.

The repair of the soul occurs on a different timeline than ours. So, exercise some self-control and trust that solutions will present themselves. Here are a few steps to get started:

1. **Recognize the shadow**

The shadow is, by its very nature, hidden or despised. It's not always easy to decipher because it's so ingrained in our psyche. As a result, healing with shadow work becomes more difficult. The first step is to recognize patterns in your life that you don't want to keep repeating. Do you keep running into the same issues or feeling the same way? By using these patterns, you can bring attention to the shadow areas.

- I'm not good enough is a common shadow belief.
- They tell me that I'm unlovable, that I'm flawed, and that my emotions aren't real.
- It is imperative that I look after those in my immediate vicinity (because I was never nurtured as a child).
- Why am I so different from everyone else?

2. Conduct a compassionate investigation

It's difficult to do shadow work while still having compassion for the subject. It's easy to place the blame on someone else or on circumstances outside of our control. We must forgive those who have hurt us in order to move on, even though it is critical to recognize the key themes that shaped us, particularly as children.

Realize how others' actions may have influenced you while keeping in mind that they were doing the best they could and were behaving from their own place of hurt in order to maintain that balance.

Journal Prompts for Working with Your Inner Child's Shadow

With some introspection and probing, an inner child's wounds can be healed. Deepening your knowledge of yourself by going beyond your daily experiences can help you become more emotionally whole in the long run.

Make use of these shadow work prompts to explore your more darker aspects of your personality. They can help you re-establish contact with your adolescent self. Also, heal any wounds that your inner child may be carrying.

A word of caution: If answering any of these questions causes you to feel overwhelmed, please stop. The questions that you aren't yet ready to answer can be skipped. It's okay to discuss them with someone who can help you answer them safely and supportively.

Before starting, make sure you have fully prepared your mind and body.

- Breathe deeply to center yourself.
- Relax and feel your feet on the floor. Do a full-body scan, and relax your mind as well.
- Begin with any of the following prompts you feel most comfortable with.

Shadow Work Prompt #1: Visualize your inner child at the age when they most needed your love and support. What are their physical characteristics? How can you explain what they're doing? Give "little you" an affirmation in writing by writing a letter. Tell them how much you care for them. Show your child you believe in them by telling them they are brave, deserving, and so on. You'll see their faces light up as you read the letter to them and they'll be smiling as well.

Shadow Work Prompt #2: Visualize your inner child going through a difficult time. Perhaps they were the victims of bullying or even fell off their bicycle. It's possible that they were harmed by someone. See what comes to mind after a few moments. Keep in mind that what happened then will not occur again. Think of yourself as a grown-up approaching your wounded inner child as you close your eyes.

- Extend your sincere apologies to them.
- Express your regrets for their difficulties.
- Offer to give them a bear hug.

Finally, give them a hug and tell them how much you appreciate them. Inform them that they are now safe and that you will continue to look after them.

Shadow Work Prompt #3: What was your favorite childhood pastime? Do you feel better or worse about yourself as a result of what happened? Do you still experience those emotions as an adult? How can you cultivate those feelings if not already there?

Shadow Work Prompt #4: Do you remember a time as a child when you were hurt by someone? Perhaps they verbally or physically assaulted you. Have you had a chance to think about it? Do you believe you're harboring resentment toward me because of this? This may be a good time to talk to a friend or family member about it.

Shadow Work Prompt #5: How functional would you say your childhood home was on a scale of 1 to 10? Do you believe you grew up in a happy household? See what your inner child thinks by tapping into it. If it wasn't that good, explain why in your essay.

Even though these inner child healing prompts are short, they'll give you a good idea of what's lurking within. For those who have been traumatized as children, talking to a professional counselor can be extremely beneficial. Emotional triggers from shadow work prompts should be dealt with by reaching out to someone who can hold space while you revisit your past and heal. Using shadow work to learn more about yourself and heal old wounds can be a very effective method.

As you continue your inner healing work, be patient with yourself and show yourself a lot of love and compassion.

Deep wounds can be left by our upbringing and can manifest themselves in behavioral and emotional patterns that even the most observant individuals may be unaware of. To uncover the unhealthy patterns we've picked up over the course of our lives, we must put in a lot of work. They may appear to be facts to us, but in reality they are erroneous notions. Because they're so deeply ingrained, you might not even be aware of the beliefs that are causing you pain.

And when you do realize them, it's difficult to comprehend the extent of the harm you've done to yourself as a result of a faulty assumption. Self-love is essential in this situation. Just accept and love your path. Move on with your life once you've forgiven yourself.

Shadow work is all about bringing to light what we'd rather keep hidden. Accepting everything that is, and then having the courage to evolve into new, more healthy patterns and beliefs is the first step toward healing oneself.

Often, the scars we carry from our childhood are the most debilitating. When we've been told we're unlovable, or that our feelings are wrong, we've carried these wounds with us because no one was there to take care of us.

Be kind to the younger version of yourself. Make a mental note to tell yourself, "I adore you and am always available to help you. You're not to blame. You have done nothing to earn this treatment. You're deserving of love, and you're going to have an amazing future." You could even see the younger version of yourself hugging the older version.

It's incredibly liberating to go back in time and shower yourself with love. There's no doubt this practice will help you in your shadow work, even if it seems a bit wacky at first. This work with your inner child is yet another tool in your toolbox.

For peace to prevail, one must learn to love everything, even the darkest parts of their journey.

In any case, the path to peace does not mean ignoring the shadows; it means shining light into even the darkest recesses of your soul so that you feel love and peace radiating from every part of you.

It is possible to change your behavior and, as a result, your life once you become aware of shadow beliefs that hinder you from fully experiencing it. Each annoyance becomes a chance to dig deeper, learn more about yourself, and heal on a deeper and deeper level as you go along. This is real peace. And for this reason, we should be thankful even on the bad days. Each dark day can be turned into an opportunity for more healing if it is handled correctly.

Chapter 5. Reparenting: Setting Boundaries

When it comes to mental health, setting limits is crucial. Boundaries provide psychological protection, as well as the ability to build or preserve our self-worth and conserve our finite energy resources. Establishing appropriate boundaries in our personal and professional lives allows us to maintain good interactions with both.

It can be frightening at first to undertake this work if you have difficulty creating boundaries because you are frightened of hurting the feelings of others. Concerns about being unwelcome, abandoned, or unwanted will surface, causing us to reevaluate our actions. When learning to create reasonable boundaries, the most difficult part is realizing that doing so will always seem wrong. Fear of intimacy, being hurt or taking a risk can make us feel as if setting more modest boundaries puts us in danger. This is especially true when dealing with excessively strict boundaries.

Protective wiring is built into our brains to shield us from harm. This can have the unintentional consequence of preventing us from fully engaging in a fruitful life on a regular basis, which is unfortunate. We must accept discomfort as part of the growth process if we are to progress. Believing uncomfortable feelings are part of growth allows us to experience other positive emotions such as resilience, confidence, fulfillment and freedom.

Instead of being burdened by the weight of our false narratives, we might get involved with the possibilities of our lives. We can acquire confidence in setting clear limits through a variety of activities and tactics. Putting up a boundary stirs up old pain from childhood and provides us a chance to deal with them, shake off bad habits, and choose a new way of behaving. A boundary also offers us a wonderful opportunity to "re-parent" oneself.

Reparenting is a psychotherapy concept that is based on the idea that we all have an inner child and an inner parent within our subconscious at the same time. If our parents were continually judging us as children, we can develop an "internal parent" who is just as harsh and severe as our real parents were when we were kids. Alternatively, if they thought our emotions were too delicate, our internal parent may feel angered and disgusted with us every time we cry.

Our parents and other family members gradually teach us as children to suppress the parts of ourselves that are deemed unacceptable. For the sake of being loved, or in some circumstances just to exist, we learn to emotionally surrender ourselves. Although we may have grown up, our abandoned inner child remains deep within us and still yearns to be loved, acknowledged and validated.

The establishment of boundaries serves as a catalyst for the reactivation of our inner child wounds, as well as a wonderful opportunity to re-parent ourselves and begin the healing process. You also become aware of your emotional activity. You are able to recognize the underlying emotion as well as any associated memories or stories. As a point of reference, the stronger the feeling or reaction, the deeper the childhood wound is said to be. Let's pretend that the fear of abandonment has been triggered in this scenario:

A particularly stressful day in the office makes you yearn to escape to the couch with your significant other in order to feel at ease. You have a minor problem, though: your partner has also had a difficult day at their job, and instead of wanting to cuddle, they are feeling apprehensive of being touched at this time. As an alternative, they are requesting some privacy and space for themselves. You have just come face to face with a boundary that your partner has established. The question is, what are you supposed to do?

Your prefrontal cortex, or thinking brain, is no longer active, and so you remind yourself to be gentle and patient with yourself.

When you have achieved this logical state, you may begin to realize that even though your partner is seeking distance, this does not imply that they have fallen out of love with you. You recognize that they are attending to their own needs in the present, just as you are, and that their actions do not negatively reflect on you or the situation.

Alternatively, you might express your appreciation for the fact that they are comfortable and open enough in the relationship to express their needs rather than suppressing them, which would lead to internal anger and suggest a dysfunctional relationship at work.

Once you've done that, direct your attention to all of the recent events that have called into question this fear-driven narrative. You remember every time your partner made an effort to reach out to you, every time they showed affection for you, and every time they demonstrated their love for you. As a result, you're gain a better understanding of the whole scope of the relationship, rather than just the painful and stimulated feelings you're experiencing at the moment.

Once your discomfort level has decreased to a manageable level, the next step is to sit down and start journaling so that you can go deeper into your feelings. These feelings could be a result of the desire to be listened to and acknowledged. If your emotional trigger hasn't decreased after several sincere attempts to meet your own requirements, talk to your partner about your feelings and see if they'd be willing to offer comfort and support for a short time.

Despite the importance of others' boundaries and doing our own inner work, asking for help when needed is also acceptable. It's important to keep in mind that this should not become a regular requirement, but should only be used when you've exhausted all other options and are in desperate need of help. This extra comfort or support is usually readily available from our companions, as long as we are also ready to respect their limits as well.

Because of this circumstantial reaction of not feeling loved, we need a step-by-step process for dealing with a reopened childhood wound.

We are essentially re-parenting our inner child through this process, as we use sympathy and tolerance instead of anger (or even disgust) to connect with them. Self-soothing skills are being taught to our inner child in order to make them less reliant on external sources of comfort. To help our inner child, we must teach him or her to think objectively when faced with a difficult situation, and to focus on being grateful instead of angry. Also, we are educating our inner child on the importance of forgiving their parents and other authority figures in our lives.

We're telling our inner child that when our own resources run low, it's okay to ask for assistance from others. Over time, our inner child accepts that they can rely on our adult selves to care for them, and as a result, their internal objections begin to fade. When faced with adversity, our ability to recover increases.

The following is a simple approach to understanding the steps for re-parenting:

- Take a step forward into awareness.
- Set a compassionate intention for yourself.
- Maintain logic, while self-soothing your senses.
- Make use of the rationale and create justifying statements.
- Choose appreciation above resentment in your life.
- Increase your awareness of the broader scope.
- If required, keep a journal.

As a result of this reparenting exercise, we are encouraged to be more creative, break free from our routines, and practice self-love. The experience of crossing our partner's boundaries or discovering how to set our own can be beneficial for both.

It is not enough to simply undertake internal work on oneself to bring about inner child healing. To prevent the progress you have made in integrating your inner child from being undermined by others, you must safeguard your personal boundaries.

What are Personal Boundaries and How Do They Work?

The ability to maintain healthy connections is a crucial requirement for personal satisfaction. Personal boundaries should be established and maintained, since failing to do so or maintaining shaky personal boundaries only serve to enable unhealthy relationships that are incompatible with personal satisfaction and correspond to unhappiness.

If you think about a boundary as a protective wall, it's similar to a line of defense, or a stone wall that protects you. Protecting these aspects of yourself are considered non-negotiable if you don't want to put your mental health, emotional well-being, or physical health at risk.

In the absence of clear boundaries, you allow everyone else to treat you whatever they want, giving them consent to treat you poorly. It is your underlying principles that serve as the foundation of your personal boundaries. Being unable to set or maintain them is an act of negligence, since you are disregarding your own requirements in order to satisfy others.

Your core values should be defined as the most important things to you, and you shouldn't compromise on them.

What are the five most important values to you, and why do you believe they are important?

Most of the time, we establish shaky boundaries because our self-esteem can get so low that we put other people's desires ahead of our own. Maintaining personal boundaries while standing firm when others attempt to break through them will undoubtedly improve your sense of self-worth as you work with your inner child.

Being Self-Protective in Unhealthy Relationships

Setting limits is challenging when dealing with toxic or manipulative individuals. It's important to keep your distance from people who are draining your energy. However, as we are all aware, things aren't often as simple as they seem. It's the same with people that take advantage of you because they don't respect your boundaries.

Even if a toxic individual is a member of your own family, limit your contact with him or her for your own wellbeing. You'll be able to spot behavior that is unhealthy for you more easily as your inner child heals. If you don't want to be exploited, you need to master self-control.

The following list of behaviors are signs that your personal boundaries are weak or non-existent:

- Making choices is difficult for you.
- You don't believe in your own abilities and instead let others use them to their advantage.
- Other people frequently make you feel used.
- When others misbehave, you provide excuses for it.
- The emotional reserves you've built up are depleted, but you may still feel depressed or anxious.
- You're believe that people don't value your opinion.
- Saying 'no' makes you feel bad because you lack self-confidence.
- It's difficult for you to put your thoughts and feelings into words. It's possible that you have difficulty figuring out your true feelings about a specific situation.
- You engage in passive-aggressive behavior.
- Despite your desire to please others, you are afraid of being left behind because of your tendencies.
- In spite of your inner fury, you keep it bottled up. Even when people treat you unfairly, you don't defend yourself. You choose to ignore your gut feelings.
- When you think about how others perceive you, it makes you feel sick to your stomach.
- You find yourself in toxic or dysfunctional friendships.
- You're generally uncomfortable being yourself in front of others.

While there are numerous other warning signs to be aware of, this is only a sampling. Relationships can be stressful, but the key is to observe them objectively and figure out why you're upset. Also, refrain from making excuses for the other person's bad behavior.

Shaky boundaries can be seen in the following situations:

- Although you've been in a relationship for quite some time, your partner won't commit, so you stay with them. This shows that you put the wants and needs of another person before your own. The only thing this will do for you is cause you more hurt in the long run.

- Despite your belief that you aren't ready, you feel compelled to have a physically intimate relationship with someone. If this is the case, you may feel compelled to participate in activities in which you have no interest because of your partner's demands. Thus, even if it means damaging your own self-esteem, you find yourself caving in to their demands to appease them or remain civil in your relationship. Even though you know what you're doing is wrong and uncomfortable, you still do it.

You'll have to put in some effort if your current limitations are weak, but it will be well worth it in the long term. If you practice setting personal boundaries, you'll be able to avoid poisonous relationships and instead attract positive ones. Gaining respect from another is a byproduct of respecting yourself.

If you begin inner child work with the intention of healing, but fail to establish and maintain personal boundaries, you may encounter difficulties.

Another way of putting it is that by restoring your inner child, you risk losing the love and acceptance you've acquired. As a result, you'll be more open to mistreatment and manipulation.

Boundaries might be difficult to define and enforce on your first attempt because of opposition from others.

Setting Your Boundaries Step-by-Step

Step 1: Recognize your personal limitations.

Your boundaries are unique because they are based on your wants and needs. Doing exactly what others want indicates that your personal boundaries are either nonexistent or inadequate. Identifying and aligning your boundaries is the initial step in resolving this issue.

The examples of appropriate personal limits provided below can help you get started if you're stuck:

- I won't engage in romantic relations with someone if they are married, already attached, or emotionally unavailable for at least two months to avoid establishing false beliefs of a connection with that person.
- No one has the right to force me to give up any of my other connections or long term goals for the sake of another.
- I won't allow myself to be ridiculed, either privately or publicly, for being the real me.
- I won't put up with a romantic partner lying or cheating.

There is no need to explain your reasoning to anyone once a boundary has been established. Your very existence indicates the importance you attach to having a boundary.

Step 2: Draw clear lines delineating your territory.

The more explicit and extensive the barrier, the more effective it will be to keep it in place in the future. Personal boundaries can be thought of as a rulebook you've created just for you, and breaching those rules will make you feel discomfort and unhappiness.

Pulling away shows the other individual that you've established boundaries. Either they accept it or they don't have you. It is absolutely up to them whether or not they react in a certain way. When you forsake your own boundaries for someone else, you relinquish authority to them. This will not establish a healthy relationship; rather, it will create a poisonous connection that will be exceedingly destructive to you.

Step 3. Personal boundaries should be a part of every day life.

If you prefer to type it out and have it printed, make a list of your desired personal limits. You should read them once per day, if not more often. Accept, as you read them, that you are worthy of others respecting your limits and that you are worthy of such consideration. Continue this exercise until they become ingrained in your consciousness, and then re-read them to serve as a reminder that you are empowered.

Step 4: Make a commitment to maintaining your personal boundaries.

This is the point at which you must be bold, because you will face people who will try to break through your barricades. This is precisely the time when you must be confident, not but confrontational.

Simply declare 'No' in a calm manner. You are not under any obligation to justify yourself, and you do not owe anyone anything. However, it is your responsibility to guard your own self-respect. Never, ever compromise on your own personal values.

Maintaining your personal boundaries becomes easier the more you do it. Make a commitment to this behavior. If someone crosses any of your limits, make sure they know there will be consequences for their actions. This will demonstrate to them that you are serious about your self-respect and that you will preserve your boundaries at any price.

Consider your long-term well-being when dealing with a manipulative or toxic individual you still care about.

Create a list of the things that you desire and need within a relationship, such as love, compassion, respect and loyalty. This will make it easy to compare your expectations with the truth of your partnership. Unless these two things are in alignment, it's generally best to leave.

Understand that a manipulative or toxic individual may begin with a tiny goal in mind, such as attempting to break through a small boundary. They are putting you through a test, and allowing them to cross even minor boundaries puts you at risk for much more serious difficulties later on.

Step 5: Re-examine your personal limits.

After you have created and enforced your boundaries, you should examine them on a regular basis. You will continue to learn during your life, and as a result, your boundaries can shift. Be accepting of this possibility. What worked for you when you were 26 may not work for you when you are 36. Examine and analyze your own boundaries on a regular basis. Do you feel at ease around these limits? Do they serve your interests well, yet are still beneficial to others?

A profound feeling of empowerment comes from setting and maintaining personal boundaries. Your sense of worth and self-assurance will soar. It's safe to continue working with your inner kid. Your journey to becoming a healthy, joyful, and well-balanced individual will be well under way once you put this into practice. If you fail to maintain a specific boundary, don't condemn yourself. Don't criticize yourself or feel inadequate because you are learning; be patient and persistent in your efforts, and it will become easier.

Chapter 6. Your Inner Child And Relationships

However old we are at this particular moment in time, our inner child can push us backwards to a younger level of emotional maturity in order to deal with challenging daily situations. Negative childhood memories are frequently carried and hidden by the inner child, and regardless of how emotionally evolved we believe we are, our adult selves frequently require assistance in addressing and resolving past traumas and traumatic events.

During childhood, this younger half of us frequently loses the ability to express himself or herself authentically. Consequently, the child is forced to meet their basic physical and emotional requirements on their own, and they are deprived of the wonderful opportunity to simply be a child. The traumas and abuse we encounter as children within our Families of Origin, as well as the wounds they leave behind, might prevent us from acting appropriately during emotionally charged life events as adults. We allow the younger aspects of ourselves to take control and attempt to settle adult concerns through the eyes of a hurt child.

What if your inner child is causing problems in your relationship?

In situations where you respond in a way that is self-destructive or negative, it is beneficial to ask yourself, "How old am I feeling right now?" Assuming your answer is that you are feeling emotionally younger than your actual age, you may be on your way to recognizing the unmet needs that you are seeking to meet with the current activity that you are engaging in. Unmet childhood and adult demands are frequently similar, if not identical, in nature. For many adults, growing up without a joyful, stable, and loving childhood is a reality of life that must be accepted.

Take a few moments to consider the following questions:

- What is the current situation of your romantic life?
- Do you have a history of romantic partners who have unconditionally loved and supported you without reservation?
- Or is there a lot of turbulence and grief in your history with others?

Our relationships can become toxic and stagnant if we continue to take our shattered inner child along with us. Your inner child is patiently awaiting the conclusion of the conflict and the restoration of peace. When you give it to them, you will notice a shift in your interpersonal interactions.

How Your Inner Child Can Wreck A Relationship

Our inner child exists in a constant state of fear; they are trapped in the moment when they were so emotionally broken that they didn't know where to go for help. They will follow us from relationship to relationship until we can discover the strength to heal and comfort this child within ourselves. It is important for you to let go of the past and find the strength to go forward in life.

Personal development and self-healing are always discussed in terms of the inner child, which is a common theme in the field. However, a significant portion of it revolves around a story that is quite transient. We can't simply acknowledge our inner child and then move on from the experience. We must incorporate them into our life — not just in a particular instance, but throughout the course of our existence.

It is common for the inner child to remain hidden under all of the chaos that comes with living in a condition of perpetual conflict, poisonous behaviors, and skillful manipulation. If you want to be in relationships that bring you peace, you must be willing to open up to them and allow them to open up to you in all of their hurt and pain.

The following behaviors and patterns are the most common signs of our inner child sabotaging our relationships:

Conflict has increased in intensity.

Is there tension in every relationship you've ever been in? Is it common for you to throw tantrums when you don't get your way with your significant other? Do you refuse to look for a middle ground or do you insist on having your way all of the time?

A child's demands are those where they are urgently trying to carve out a place for themselves in the world. When we allow our inner child to grow away from fears of loss and fears of being seen, we can lessen our desire for confrontation and hence our stress levels.

Patterns become toxic.

Every day, the inner child is attempting to understand and justify the trauma that has been inflicted upon them. When it comes to relationships, this is most often manifested in your actions and beliefs. If you have a toxic pattern of chasing down unavailable relationships, it is possible that you are chasing individuals who remind you of the monster who used to live under your bed. A fear of being abandoned may also cause you to become overly attached to others. Because of our damaged inner child and the grief we refuse to let go, these abusive behaviors thrive in us.

Manipulation is done with finesse.

Children don't have a lot of influence in today's society. In reality, the majority of parents prefer their children to remain silent at all times, regardless of the situation. This instills in children the belief that they are unable to communicate directly with their parents. As our inner children grow up, they learn that emotional manipulation is the most effective approach to acquire what they want from others. This includes everything from being dismissive to outright denial. This, however, may often lead to micromanipulation and toxic relationships in which we manipulate and harass our partners rather than being honest with them.

The inner child creates suppressed feelings.

What is the current status of your emotions when it comes to your interpersonal interactions? Are you stable and aware of your surroundings? Or do you want to share stories about considerably more serious issues with those around you? Broken inner children aid us in the creation of distorted closeness. We struggle with dealing with our emotions, or even processing them on a personal level. The majority of the time, we suppress our feelings and bury them. We would rather keep our delusions alive than find satisfaction in the reality of our situation.

Honesty is avoided.

Consider your own childhood experiences. Was there anything that happened when you made a blunder or broke something you weren't allowed to? Did you flee and take cover? Most likely you were avoiding repercussions.

The same can be said for your inner child. When we allow this inner version of ourselves to go unchecked for an extended period of time, they learn to avoid honesty, and so do we. This avoidance manifests itself in our relationships, as well as in our failure to stand up when it matters the most.

Your relationships are a revolving door.

Do you have a revolving door of relationships in your life? Perhaps you're trying to figure out what you want, or you're having trouble finding someone who "makes sense." While using this technique may appear to be logical, it does not add up if you have never spent any time thinking about what is important and what is not. We must first heal and find peace within ourselves, rather than passing through one person after another and damaging so many lives in the process.

The past becomes a hindrance to the present

Does the thought of your partner abandoning you fill you with dread? Do you get agitated when someone does not respond to your text message immediately? It's possible that it has absolutely nothing to do with what's going on with them right now in your life. It's possible that your anxieties arise from a difficult childhood.

Adults who feel secure in their romantic relationships are more likely to describe early connections with their parents as being warm, kind, and accepting. Those who have experienced a traumatic upbringing, on the other hand, develop unstable attachments.

If you grew up with a parent who was negligent, inconsistent, or abusive, or if you lost a parent through death or divorce, you may be experiencing abandonment difficulties. It was discovered in a 2010 study titled "Quality of Social Relationships and the Development of Depression in Parentally-Bereaved Youth" that abandonment concerns following the loss of a parent can have an impact on subsequent relationships with partners. Even years after the incident, your inner child can still react at the most inconvenient times – whenever someone in your life pushes your buttons.

The Healing Process for Better Connections

Inner wounds seldom heal for individuals who have been emotionally and mentally harmed during their childhood.

In addition to experiencing temper tantrums and having difficulty making friends, the child may be skeptical of the motivations of others and may engage in other disruptive behaviors. As these emotionally injured children get older, they are able to shed some of their childhood behaviors, but the wounded inner child remains buried deep within their mind. When these individuals are frustrated, under pressure, or starting to feel overwhelmed, they frequently revert to their old behavior patterns and the tactics they used to get their way as children.

A wounded inner child may also crave attention and connection that they never experienced outside of their family or home. These individuals may tolerate toxic, destructive, and abusive behavior in a relationship.

It is essential that you let your inner child heal if you want to have a more secure, fair, and healthy connection with others. This is not a straightforward procedure. It is also not a one-size-fits-all solution or something that can be completed in one day. You must first embrace who your inner child is, and then you must create an environment in which they can feel secure to express themselves. You must also involve your partners in the healing process and devise more effective methods of letting go of the past and accepting where you are now.

1. Acknowledge that you have an inner child.

The acceptance of one's situation is the first step in any healing process. You won't be able to get where you want to go until you know exactly where you are now. You must first admit that your inner child exists and that they have been legitimately suffering for the majority of your life. And it is through this process that we are able to move into reality and out of the terrible delusions that we have been living in. The moment we accept our inner child for who they truly are, we open the door and allow them to enjoy the fresh air and sunshine for the first time.

Would you turn a blind eye to a weeping child on the side of the road? Empathy and compassion for your inner child should be applied in the same way. Admitting that something is wrong with you on the inside does not imply that you are less deserving. You will get stronger as a result of it. Once you have acknowledged the existence of your inner child, you can acknowledge their experiences, identify the lessons they have learned, and let go. Furthermore, you can find tranquility in your own life and connect with a future that you had never considered possible before.

2. Involve your partner in the healing process.

It's difficult to start a new life with someone while still going through a significant healing process. This is due to the fact that healing is difficult. It brings with it happy days, but it also brings with it difficult days. Your spouse becomes a witness to what is taking place. They are there to watch your suffering with your inner child, and they are there to witness your triumph over that anguish. It is impossible to avoid having your partner as a witness, no matter how much you wish.

When you're in recovery, it's critical to communicate with your partner. Obviously, this does not imply that we must reveal the full extent of our difficulties. We should, however, feel comfortable in informing them that we are working on something. And it's perfectly fine to anticipate their compassion.

Don't cross any lines you're not completely comfortable with. However, being concerned about sharing personal healing with your partner is a major red flag. When we share something important with someone we care about, we should not be embarrassed to tell them about it. To be honest, when we are matched with the right people, they will love and support us through this task, even if they don't understand or aren't privy to what we're doing. Allow your partner to participate in your healing to the extent you are comfortable with, and share in your joy as your condition improves.

3. Provide a safe environment for your inner child to exit.

Our inner child exists primarily in a state of fear. They were marked by emotionally distressing incidents at critical junctures in their development. These traumas cause them to be cautious to open up, and even more unwilling to break free from the habits and harmful beliefs that have kept them hidden for so long. They must, however, be brought to light. Consequently, it is our responsibility to provide a safe environment in which people feel comfortable communicating with us and sharing their experiences.

Give yourself permission to allow your inner child to come out and stretch their legs in both life and love. You need to console them and accept them on a personal level in order to help them heal. Aside from that, you must make certain that the partners you choose provide a safe environment for them to feel wanted, healed, and complete again.

Allow your inner child to express their feelings. When you begin to feel the anguish mounting, take a step back and allow it to wash over you. Allow them to share their memories and all of the negative experiences that have occurred in their lives. Set a time restriction for yourself. When the time is up, softly take their hands in yours and guide them away to something exciting and distracting. Keep a journal of your experience. You will gradually see a child who is becoming more and more confident in holding your hand in his or hers and adoring you in return.

4. Improve your ability to re-parent yourself.

Broken inner children are frequently the result of traumatized parents who instilled trauma in them, both intentionally and unintentionally. In order for us to be the parents that these inner children never had, we must step in and take on the role of their parents.

Re-parent yourself in the proper manner. Examine your inner child with candor, and pay attention to the habits and belief systems that are having the most impact on your overall quality of life. How can you convince them that loving someone is a safe thing to do? How can you teach them to quit lashing out at the world and the people who really matter in their lives.

Be the empathetic ear they've never heard from in their lives. Remove all of the judgments and all of the fear that has kept them from moving forward. Demonstrate to them what it means to be a responsible caregiver. Demonstrate to them that someone appreciates them exactly as they are; someone who does not require them to perform in order to receive love or acceptance. Make sure to set clear boundaries for them and to be firm, but in the most loving way possible.

5. Assist your inner child in letting go of the past.

The inner child, more than anything else, dwells in this space between our present and our former selves. They lash out at us in the present, yet their memories and feelings are firmly rooted in the traumatic experiences of our recent past. In order for us to be able to go on, we must first extract this inner child from the past and firmly plant them in the present. After all, they have earned the right to celebrate their recovery. Teach them how to learn from their mistakes and move on so that they can eventually be happy in their lives.

Help your inner child let go of the past and all of the relationships and people who have mistreated them while they were growing up there. It was not their fault that this happened. They were unable to influence the actions of those in their immediate vicinity, nor did they do anything to encourage such behavior.

Create an environment in which your inner child can feel safe and secure enough to let go and have fun. Believe in your ability to live without all of the agony and all of the wrath following you around. Entice them into the future by providing them with all of the possibilities of what is to come. You can still experience the affection that your inner child yearns for. Total and unwavering acceptance can be found in a selected family and partners who will accept you for who you are, no matter how little your stature.

Accept the fact that you have an inner child and acknowledge the grief that they have experienced. Ensure that they are welcomed into a safe environment by cultivating relationships with compassionate others. Especially if you're in a significant or long-term relationship, it's important to include your spouse or partner in the healing process in any way you feel comfortable. This could be as basic as a passing comment or as extensive as active participation.

Our inner children exist trapped in a state of limbo between childhood and adulthood. When we find ourselves in toxic relationships for an extended period of time, it's typically because of this inner child and the suffering they're still experiencing. In order for us to discover pleasure and a deeper connection in our relationships, we must first accept the anguish our inner children are experiencing and the harm they are causing to our lives as a result. Then we can take them by the hand and muster up the strength to assist them in their recovery.

Chapter 7. The Inner Child And Your Career

As you have learned, the inner child in our psyche serves as a reminder of who we were as children. Approximately 90% of the time, it contains our beliefs about ourselves, and it controls our sub-conscious behavior at home, when traveling, and of course while at work.

Childhood trauma, also known as Adverse Childhood Experiences (ACEs), will have left an imprint on your impressionable inner child, which will be difficult to erase. It is a psychological wound that continues to bleed in the present day. We may see the effects of our traumas in every facet of our lives. Even though your inner child has not been hurt at work, it will manifest itself there, influencing your judgments and behaviors, and ultimately your job and business relationships.

The Wounded Inner Child And Professional Performance

With a wounded inner child, you experience the feeling of being unqualified, incompetent, and prone to 'get it wrong.' Making decisions or taking action is avoided because of the fear of making a mistake and appearing silly or failing.

You may continue to put off doing something until it is absolutely perfect - which it will never be. One of the most common reasons for procrastination is the inability to complete a task. The effort and contribution you make to the team begin to feel inadequate, which is essentially a reflection of an incorrect self-perception.

Along with this, you might have an excessive sensitivity to criticism or 'feedback'. Hiding behind the ego is a protective mechanism that keeps you from feeling vulnerable to humiliation and inferiority. You keep your thoughts and feelings contained within your head to prevent being affected by your heart. You may find yourself being a people pleaser and being overly compliant. This might lead to instances in which you are treated with contempt by colleagues, and you may even become the target of derision or disdain. You are ultimately afraid of being shamed and 'put down' by others, thus you are not willing to risk sharing your own identity through thoughts or preferences.

When the inner child is not addressed, it is also quite easy to become overwhelmed and burnt out if you are not in touch with your own needs and do not practice self-care on a regular basis. Working excessively hard for an extended period of time can result in health problems that are subsequently ignored. Failure is something a wounded inner child fears and your 'ego identity' must be fiercely safeguarded from any potential shame or exposure as a result of your failure.

Other common examples of dysfunction in the workplace include the following:

- You will avoid delegation and collaboration at all costs. You will strive to handle everything yourself and will not trust others to assist you or to do it "right" for you.
- You put blame on external factors such as the economy, the government, coworkers, and competitors for any failure.
- You put on a show of bravado and seem to be superior in order to conceal the inner child's true feelings of helplessness and inferiority.
- You suffer from the sensation that one is being exposed as a fraud, also known as Imposter Syndrome.
- You have intense rage at authority figures combined with a refusal to follow the rules – this is the rebellious inner child in action.
- In order to prevent feeling vulnerable, you may overcompensate for your fears and doubts by becoming an autocratic and inflexible narcissist who is distant, aloof, and bullying to others' feelings in order to avoid feeling vulnerable.

Another issue that often goes unnoticed is that you may also still be dominated by your prior parent-child dynamics. Your 'inner critical parent' can manifest itself in the office or workplace where it keeps your inner child suppressed and on the verge of proving their worth to the world. The inability to rise above your parent's or your siblings' level of accomplishment is a source of frustration. You maintain a reduced self-image in order to please and soothe the egos of family members. This fear of standing out, speaking up, and making a difference is prevalent, even when you know you have something valuable to offer that others desire and need.

The development of "fighter's mentality" may prompt you to be overly eager to challenge and defend your position – or any perceived threat to that position. Your desire to avoid the expected agony and humiliation of being attacked or belittled in any way drives you to overreact in this manner. You want to 'get in there first' in case something goes wrong.

Emotional Intelligence & The Inner Child

Another common issue in the workplace is a failure to communicate or understand a colleague's communication due to a lack of emotional intelligence (EQ). If you were emotionally mistreated as a child, it is possible that you would struggle to comprehend and express your feelings, which is known as Alexithymia, as an adult. This results in poor leadership messaging, weaker team cohesion and a lack of suitable emotional attunement to staff needs.

Your need to be liked and popular may lead to a lack of self-control and the establishment of weak and loose boundaries – such as being excessively pleasant, sending inappropriate or muddled messages, and engaging in inappropriate flirting or harassing behavior.

Overall, you aren't free to simply get on with your work and do your best to complete the task at hand. While on the job, your emotional traumas are being re-activated, and you are no longer functioning from your more stable, dependable, and capable adult state of mind.

Healing The Inner Child At Work

Having a content inner child who does not feel the need to behave in the ways described above will instead free up a tremendous quantity of good energy and reap tremendous benefits, including:

- Creativity that comes naturally
- Perceiving the wider picture and having access to broader perspectives and connecting topics
- The enjoyment of light-hearted conversation and laughter with colleagues, without any underlying agenda
- Demonstrating modesty and humility, as well as setting aside and dedicating time to others
- The ability to be calm, confident, and emotionally aware in the face of adversity
- Being content with being a successful boss or employee
- Being constantly on the lookout for and acquiring new ideas and concepts

It is essential that you listen to customers and your staff in order to better understand their needs. The inner child is driven by a natural sense of curiosity and a desire to form relationships with others.

That being said, it's important to take a break from acting like an adult every now and then, and accept that you will never know everything. Bringing a light hearted attitude to the office isn't an excuse for employees to skip work, as is commonly believed. It increases productivity and can put you in a flow state, which is when you're totally focused on something that's both difficult and creatively engaging at the same time.

Here are some suggestions for bringing out your inner child at work:

1. Enquire about things

There's no denying that children look to adults as the source of all knowledge. If you've ever seen a child go through a 'But, why?' rabbit hole, you understand precisely what I mean. Take a break from acting like an adult every now and then, and accept that you will never know everything. Asking questions can help you come up with a solution because it's okay to confess you don't have all the answers. Try asking open-ended questions like: "What appears to be the problem?", "What else do I need to know about this?" and "What's holding our team back from succeeding?"

2. Make your work more fun by using games.

As wonderful motivators for children to learn, reward charts in academic contexts are ubiquitous, but this may also be implemented in modern companies. Let's say you have a mountain of tedious paperwork to get through. Why not make it a two-person race, with the loser having to foot the bill for the other person's coffee? Consider setting a deadline and then going to your favorite sandwich shop for lunch. Try to walk 2,000 steps a day or take brief meditation breaks with your coworkers to help you achieve your health and well-being goals.

3. Meet new people.

Isn't it fascinating how adept children are at forming new friendships? They don't hesitate to welcome newcomers into their area to converse or participate in activities. Adults, on the other hand, are a whole distinct species. A study published in Social Psychological and Personality Science found that small talk improved executive functioning, the part of the brain associated with focus, prioritization, and organization, thus reaching out to a coworker may be the key to enhancing job satisfaction. Consider what your inner child would do the next time you avoid an after-work event.

4. Have a sense of curiosity

We're indoctrinated to be curious and to make mistakes as children. Everyone on the planet has had to go through a period of mumbling before learning to talk. No one had learned how to walk without tripping and stumbling all over the place. Curiosity always trumps ego when you're a kid, so be open to the possibility of failure when trying new activities. This means that cultivating an inquisitive mind doesn't necessitate taking on intimidating tasks. Even something as basic as changing the time you have lunch might lead to unexpected encounters, such as listening to a fascinating radio show or running into an old friend. Consider taking on a new project or volunteering for a position you've never had before.

No one ever truly grows up, at least not in the traditional sense. No matter how hard somebody tries, some aspect of their childhood self will always be present. Some people may not consider this to be a positive characteristic to possess in themselves. Let's face it, children aren't typically regarded as being the most wise or the most capable decision makers in the world. However, there is one characteristic of a child that only an idiot would fail to see or would choose to overlook. This is due to the fact that children learn more quickly than their adult counterparts on an innate level. Every day is a new learning experience for them, so it's very evident why an older person will be unable to compete in this environment.

It's difficult not to have come face to face with your inner child if you're a successful professional in your chosen area. Anyone's inner child becomes most visible to the outside world when what they're doing no longer appears to be work. Pursuing further knowledge in this field seems to be the most entertaining idea that has ever occurred to them.

When we were younger, our ideas of what an ideal adult life would be were founded on the ability to earn a living doing something that we found enjoyable at the time. It's no surprise that the majority of children aspire to be professional athletes or performers. The folks they saw all the time doing what they enjoyed and leading high-quality lives as a result of doing it on a professional level were the ones they admired.

Examine your progress and the distance you've traveled.

Everyone with even a sliver of significant experience in any industry will tell you that the finest moments were always in the beginning, when everything was new and unknown. Let us not forget the uncertain destination, the seemingly insurmountable aims, the unimaginably arduous learning curve and, of course, the financial struggles. Taking a few seconds to reflect on where you are now in relation to where you were when you first started will help you have a greater appreciation for what you have and the road that has brought you to this point.

The person who was discovered in childhood youth is never fully gone once the process of maturation begins. It merely shifts from awareness to the subconscious mind, where it awaits the opportunity to be of help once more. Finding a vocation in which discovering your inner child is a breeze is critical to maintaining one's sanity for any professional in a competitive field.

What you should take away from this is that as you grow older, your inner child will start to show in your unconscious behaviors. These have the ability to affect your life and create self-fulfilling prophecies.

You have the option of interpreting these prophecies as either beneficial or detrimental to your life. You are the only person who can truly connect with and commit to mending your inner child, as well as to accepting responsibility for 're-parenting' them and meeting their future ongoing needs, thus healing their earlier emotional wounds and reestablishing your own sense of self.

Chapter 8. The Inner Child And Your Finances

Do you toss and turn in your sleep at night, worrying about your finances? Or are you a superb saver who doesn't let money stress you out?

As it turns out, the origins of your current ideas and money habits may be traced all the way back to your earliest years of development. If you look far enough into your past, you will discover the reasons why you are either succeeding or struggling in your financial life.

Whether we are aware of it or not, how we were raised has a significant impact on the decisions we make as young adults and adults. Positive outcomes do occur from time to time, however, there are times when the outcomes are damaging to our well-being, particularly when it comes to our financial health. This does not imply that we can just point the finger at our parents for our financial missteps and call it a day. Once we grasp the underlying causes of our harmful habits, we must accept responsibility for them and make a concerted attempt to change them.

In spite of this, we frequently forget that our inner child, the formerly traumatized child, is aroused by the stresses of today's life. The circumstances in the present amplify any past traumas that resulted in the needs of our inner child not being met.

Early childhood trauma may cause us to unwittingly turn to our partners, our careers, and other people to "fix" our difficulties rather than look within. We look to the outside world to offer us with the emotional, spiritual, or monetary requirements that we either did not receive or received at a high cost as a result of our upbringing. Without a doubt, this is an unrealizable expectation. Instead of confronting the initial hurt, we "project" our parents' original hopes onto others rather of confronting the underlying hurt. It was the original hope that someone would come to our aid in order to assure our survival because we couldn't. Current concerns about one's ability to "survive" in "these times" rekindle the memories of the past pain. And it's possible that it's turning up right now for a reason. Perhaps this is the best moment to investigate it.

Consider your earliest recollection that has anything to do with money. It could have been as simple as putting pennies in a piggy bank, spending your allowance, or accompanying your parents to the bank to start a savings account with them. What is the first thing that comes to mind when you think of money?

What was your first-hand encounter with money like? Perhaps you were given an allowance and your family instructed you on how to make prudent financial and spending decisions. Or did your parents simply present you with everything they wished you to have because you didn't have an allowance?

After considering these questions, have a look at each of your parents. What were some of the lessons you took away from them? It's possible that they never discussed money at all, and you've come to associate money with concealment. Or embarrassment. Or they may have planted subtle bombs that crept into your consciousness, such as "Rich people are greedy"; "Money is the foundation of all evil"; or "Always present the appearance of having a lot of money."

There may have been a specific incident that precipitated the change, such as a funeral, divorce, or job loss. The cumulative effect of all of these events imprinted your brain with your money views and shaped the way you operate today. If you were raised with the belief that it is essential to demonstrate to the world that you are successful, it is likely that you will spend more money than you should in order to live up to that expectation.

Is this to say that you're trapped with whatever ideas about money that you were provided in your childhood? Not in the least. As soon as your money beliefs no longer serve your ideals in the adult world, you should replace them with something more appropriate. You begin by acknowledging that just because a message was absorbed by your child-mind does not imply that it should be a part of your current existence.

Reframing Learned Money Behaviors

Here are eight common parenting behaviors that can have a detrimental impact on your financial habits, as well as what you can do to avoid or overcome these tendencies.

1. Your parents were extremely frugal in their spending.

When it came to your behavior, your parents seemed to deny you of anything you wanted as a child, whether it was because they were attempting to teach you a lesson or simply because they wanted to put their own financial interests first.

The Learned Habit

You overpay in order to make up for lost time. Binge spending is frequently triggered by a sense of deprivation experienced as a child.

The Solution

Hasn't everyone read about the stern parents whose rogue child ended up going haywire? Perhaps your parents' frugality is causing you to behave inappropriately with your financial decisions. The solution is to talk to your parents about their decisions and the reasons behind them. It's possible that there's more to their choices than you realized when you were younger. Whatever you do, remember that the only true restitution for childhood deprivation is financial prosperity. Channel your inner rebel as much as you can in order to conserve money rather than spend it. If your willpower isn't strong enough to keep you from overspending, force yourself to do so by setting up automatic savings programs whenever it is practical.

For parents, it's important to explain your financial prudence to your children, so they don't become resentful and miss out on learning the value of saving.

2. Your parents were extremely generous individuals.

Perhaps your parents were raised in poverty or were directly subjected to trauma. As a result, they decided to devote their time and resources to causes that they were passionate about.

The Learned Habit

Your heart is in the right place, as was your mother and father's before you. However, you may feel compelled to give more money than you can realistically afford to do so out of guilt or responsibility. Donating to charitable causes is difficult to resist, whether as a result of your own experience or a desire to equal your parents' level of generosity. Charity is a lovely and noble notion, but it is easy to let your emotions get the better of you, which can result in you saying "yes" to too many requests and donating more money than you can afford in the long run.

The Solution

Determine which causes are most important to you and create a charitable donation budget for the next year that is within your financial means now. This budget should leave a little wiggle allowance in case any unexpected events come up that you might like to support. Set up monthly or annual recurring payments to the charity organizations of your choice through your bank, and notify the organizations of your plans. Thus, you will be less motivated to give excessively as a result of emotional or impulse driven giving because you will know exactly what you are giving and when you are giving it.

3. Your parents gave you a lot of privileges.

Consider the following: Perhaps your parents were disadvantaged as children themselves, therefore they chose to overspend on you as a result of their own hardships. You grew up in a world where there was plenty and you didn't have to worry about anything.

The Learned Habit

You believe you are entitled to live a wealthy lifestyle, which you do. Children who have been spoiled can sometimes grow up believing that they can — and should — continue to receive whatever they desire. However, the difficulty is that you may not have enough income to fund your desire to live lavishly, which can lead to the accumulation of unneeded debt.

The Solution

The key is to shift your entitlement mindset away from having a lot of "things" now and toward financial independence later. Experiment with living modestly for a while to discover what it's like. Then use the money you save to help you achieve more significant goals such as purchasing a home, enjoying a happy retirement, or establishing a family. To push yourself to make better financial decisions for the future, set up automatic retirement payments for yourself.

4. Your parents were critical of the stock market.

Whether they experienced the Great Depression, suffered a significant loss during the Great Recession, or made poor stock-picking judgments in the past, your parents have opted to store their money in the safest possible location: under the bed.

The Learned Habit

The result of this impact is that you refrain from investing in stocks completely. However, while stashing your cash appears to be a secure alternative, the reality is that you must maximize the growth of your funds in order to have any hope of living comfortably in retirement. With the exception of stock and real estate investments, your options are limited.

The Solution

The remedy is to exercise caution and foresight while making investment decisions. This is conducting sufficient study and asking pertinent questions, if necessary, to ensure that you understand what you're getting yourself into and that it is acceptable for your aims and risk tolerance. You should also make certain that your overall investment portfolio is well-diversified in order to avoid exposing yourself to unneeded risk.

5. Your parents lived beyond their means.

It's likely that they were acting in this manner to make up for something they had been deprived of as children, or because they wanted to keep up with their social status. Whatever the cause, your parents indulged themselves and most likely spent more money than they should have.

The Learned Habit

You, too, live beyond your financial means. Despite our best efforts, we are prone to resembling our parents on a regular basis. A more modest lifestyle would be tough for you to adopt after growing up with role models who lived in luxury. As a result, you are most likely striving to keep up with not just your peers, but also with your parents, which is a sad state of affairs to be in.

The Solution

If you are unable to physically remove yourself from an atmosphere that tempts you to overspend, then you must impose limitations on yourself in order to prevent yourself from overspending. Set up automated transfers to help you save money you'd otherwise spend, and keep a separate checking account and debit card just for everyday spending. Remove any overdraft protection.

6. Your parents have separated.

This is an unpleasant reality for so many families, and it is a significant contributor to a wide range of psychological disorders in children, including those that lead to bad financial decision-making.

The Learned Habit

Regardless of what occurs, you're going to have a "happily ever after" life. Even though this isn't necessarily a terrible thing, it can lead to you entering into a marriage, purchasing a home, and starting a family too soon or for the wrong reasons. If you live beyond your means, you may find yourself in a state of debt and experiencing financial hardship – all of which may eventually lead to divorce. The vicious loop is still in effect.

The Solution

Take time in making the big decisions. Develop a habit of thinking things through before making big purchases like a house or car.

7. Your parents did not teach you anything about money.

Having poor financial habits is a common occurrence brought on by unintentional repetitions of a parent's lack of financial literacy. Speaking of money is frowned upon because of its tarnished image as something corrupt and unsavory. Historically speaking, women have been kept in the dark regarding home finances as well, so this is nothing new for them either. As a result, generations of parents have shied away from discussing money with their children, either out of ignorance or out of preference.

The Learned Habit

You are financially illiterate – and this is likely manifested in a multitude of ways, including overspending, under saving, avoiding investing or financial planning in general, among others. Because you don't have a solid understanding of money management, you'll have to learn by making mistakes and perhaps learning from them in the future.

The Solution

The remedy is simple: educate yourself. You may also take it a step further by retaining the services of an experienced, trained financial advisor who can provide you with tailored counsel, put you on the proper path to achieving your objectives, and, ideally, educate you while you are doing so. Make use of references from relatives and friends, and interview numerous candidates until you discover one you like and can put your confidence in. If you are a parent, you should make it a priority to communicate to your children about money and involve your children in your financial planning activities so that they can stop the cycle of debt.

Creating New Money Beliefs

As an adult, do you consider yourself to be wealthy, impoverished, or somewhere in between? Do you have the impression that your friends, extended family, and classmates are in a better financial and social position than you?

The following are a few examples of how you can reconstruct your old beliefs with new ones:

- Old belief: I use money to demonstrate to others that I am successful.
- New belief: Money is something I utilize to ensure the long-term well-being of my family and myself.

- Old belief: Money is equivalent to stress.
- New belief: I need to gain a better grasp of my financial situation in order to find peace of mind in my life.

- Old belief: I don't have enough or my money's going away.
- New belief: I'm confident in my abilities to make more money if I have to.

- Old belief: Money is the root of all evil.
- New belief: Money itself is not the root of all evil, but it gives me the power to express my authenticity

- Old belief: Money is meant to be spent so let's live for the moment.
- New belief: Living for the moment will put me in a spending trap.

With commitment to improving our ideas about money, our inner child does not have to surrender to the inner parental critic. As adults we are free to establish new patterns of behavior in regards to our finances.

Making a decision to stay financially independent for the rest of your life is the answer, regardless of whether you marry or are already married. In order to accomplish this, you must maintain separate accounts for spending, saving, and investing, as well as make it a priority in your relationship to contribute as much as you possibly can to your own personal retirement account-- even if you are not the breadwinner or have left the workforce to be a caretaker. Consider a prenuptial agreement as a reasonable and protective measure if you have a substantial financial advantage over your future spouse.

If your money views have gotten out of control, you may want to explore working with a therapist who specializes in Cognitive Behavior Therapy to help you develop new habits that will allow you to live the life of your dreams. Just keep in mind that you are not tied to your prior ideas, which simply serve to prolong and reinforce your suffering. You have the potential to effect change, and you should use it to the best of your ability.

Chapter 9. Inner Child Journaling

Have you ever noticed that when you're at your lowest point, you tend to think back to situations from your past that you had to cope with as a child? Do you ever find yourself complaining not from a position of authority, but rather from the perspective of a child? Have you ever felt a little odd after an emotional outburst or a release of wrath and grief and wondered where all the resentment and pain came from?

Recovery work often brings people face to face with their inner child's restrained feelings and emotions. This is, indeed, a powerful experience. Accepting and processing these feelings and emotions needs a great deal of strength and courage. One's inner-child may be so fearful, afraid and lost that one wants to hug and not let go.

People's reactions vary when it comes to their inner-child experiences and feelings. The most important thing is to pay attention to your inner child and try to give them the comfort they seek in return. Compassion, empathy, and unconditional and limitless support are all critical components of this.

In order to assist you in feeling more aligned with and healing your inner-child, here are some writing prompts. They all have the same goal: to get you closer to your inner child by bringing back fond memories of your childhood. Some of these prompts are heavy and serious, while others are light and humorous.

Writing in a journal is a great way to work on and get to know your inner child. In order to get over trauma from your childhood, try writing it down and letting go of the emotions that go along with it. Although it is possible to heal one's inner child over time, it is important to start journaling every day in small steps until you start to see results.

Spend at least 20-30 minutes a day in solitude, writing in your journal. I recommend a place with no distractions. Make yourself at home with a pen and paper or a notebook. Here are a few pointers to help you reconnect with your playful side:

- Before you begin journaling, take a few deep breaths and close your eyes for a few minutes to visualize your inner child.
- Make an intention to learn and release something as a result of this experience.
- If you can, refrain from passing judgment on the things you get
- Listen to your inner child and honor what they say.
- Be honest with yourself.
- Take a few deep breaths after you finish writing. This will help you be more aligned with your energy.

With the following journal prompts, you can begin your inner child healing work right now.

The Most Effective Writing Prompts For Healing

1. When you were a kid, what did you like to do for fun? What was the reason for your decision to quit participating in these activities? Would you like to continue them, or would you prefer not to?

2. Describe an instance when you, as a child, felt misunderstood by someone. What would you like to say to them now?

3. What stories (books, television shows or movies) did you love as a child? What emotions did they elicit from you?

4. Express your feelings about a childhood event that you believe may have contributed to an insecurity or fear you currently have.

5. When you were a kid, what did you daydream about?

6. In elementary and middle school, who were some of your favorite instructors to have?

7. As a child, what kinds of hypothetical scenarios did you come up with when you were pretend-playing?

8. When you were a kid, where did you imagine yourself to be by now?

9. Describe a time when you were a child and felt unsafe.

10. When you were a kid, what was your favorite subject in school?

11. When you were younger, did you have a more pessimistic or more optimistic attitude on life?

12. When you were in elementary school, what was your everyday routine like when you arrived home from school?

13. Who was your childhood hero (fictional or nonfictional) and why? What was it about them that you admired?

14. Describe your closest pals from elementary and middle school, and whether or not you are still in touch with them. If your are out of touch, is there a reason you lost contact?

15. Describe a specific occurrence that you believe marked the end of your "innocence" as a youngster, a point at which you felt you had lost some of your innocence.

16. Who was the person who caused you the most pain during your childhood? Have you forgiven them yet, or do you still hold grudges against them?

17. Describe an instance when your child-self may have injured the feelings of another person.

18. What is the most difficult experience you had as a child?

19. What were some of your favorite childhood pastimes? As to why you halted these actions: Do you want to continue them? Is there a reason for this or not?

20. What were some of your favorite childhood destinations?

21. When you were a kid, where did you feel most secure?

22. When you were younger, did you have any imaginary friends? If so, how energetic were they? Pay attention to what your inner child is telling you and write it down.

23. Give an example of a time as a child when you felt misunderstood or neglected. What do you miss being able to say to them right now?

24. Do you still keep in touch with the people from your high school years? Is there a reason for this or not?

25. Write about a time in your childhood when you had self-limiting beliefs or insecurities, such as the fear of failing or thinking you were unworthy. Inquire with your inner child and find out what you can do right now to let go of your self-limiting ideas.

26. What did you want to be when you grew up? Pay attention to the messages that your inner child is trying to convey to you. Even if your childhood fantasies have changed now that you are an adult, the spirit of a child still resides within you. Explore the possibilities for achieving one's childhood aspirations. Take notes on everything.

27. Who was the person who harmed you the most as a child? Is it possible for you to forgive them at this point? Is there a reason for this or not?

28. What was the most trying experience you had as a child?

29. Give an example of a time when you may have offended someone's feelings as a child. Would your behavior toward them be different if you could go back in time? Is there a reason for this or not?

30. When you were a kid, what was your outlook on life? What do you think about that as an adult?

31. When did you feel like you'd lost your "childhood innocence"?

32. Where do you think you'd be right now if you were a kid?

33. What is the one thing that scares your inner child?

34. What would you say to your inner child if you had the chance to do so right now?

35. Is your inner child having an impact on your current life? Write down any messages your inner child sends you.

36. What can you do to show kindness and love to your inner child right now?

If you want to take the healing of your inner child to the next level, try adding color and life to your inner child's drawings in your journal. Find out what your inner child enjoys and what their favorite things are by talking to them. This can assist you in better visualizing your inner child and connecting and aligning with them.

Chapter 10. Inner Child Work: Key Takeaways

Inner child work is an important part of the developmental or transcendent process of becoming the person you know you can be. Inner child healing reconnects us to the wounded parts of our inner child. This reconnection enables you to gain access to the fractured pieces of yourself, allowing you to uncover the source of your phobias, fears, insecurities, and self-sabotaging tendencies and eliminate them.

Instead of simply identifying and addressing the symptoms of your distress, inner child healing will assist you in getting to the root of the problem and determining when it began, allowing you to deal with it more effectively. The memories of our childhood are buried deep within us, as are the lessons we learned. These recollections continue to exist and interact with the current situation. When we acknowledge this part of ourselves in our adult life, we can heal emotional difficulties that arise as a result of not honoring this part of ourselves as children. Our inner child is a source of our vitality and creativity.

Numerous pressures in our adult life threaten to extinguish the spark of our inner child, which is still alive and well within each of us. You can fight back against these influences by reconnecting with the source of your identity from infancy.

Top 5 Wounded Inner Child Traits That Deserve Your Attention

However, even though this book contains extensive information on the indicators of the wounded inner child, let's condense it into the most important points. The following are some of the most common traits:

1. **Having a highly reactive state of mind.** Our wounded inner child shows up when we overreact to situations or when we suddenly feel very alienated or frustrated in our daily lives. When this happens, we

know we have an issue. Trying to govern or control the external environment that makes us uncomfortable on the inside is what our adult selves are doing.

2. **Overestimating one's own independence.** The wounded inner child has shown defiance in seeking outside help to the detriment of their own well being. For example, you may find yourself repeating the statement "I need no one" and refuse to seek help.

3. **Engaging in self-destructive coping strategies.** This might manifest itself in the form of excessive alcohol consumption, shopping, cheating, gambling, eating, and even chronic procrastination.

4. **Displaying a lack of emotional and mental well-being.** This can manifest itself in a variety of ways, including the following:

   • Depressive symptoms
   • Feeling unmotivated
   • Wanting to spend increasing amounts of time alone
   • Not wanting to be intimate to keep a relationship going
   • Sleep disturbances
   • Gaining or losing weight
   • Being less focused and productive at work
   • Experiencing increased anxiety in several areas of one's life

5. **Recreating negative behavior patterns.** In adult relationships, whether romantic or not, people who have experienced attachment traumas are more likely to unintentionally reproduce the attachment patterns they experienced as children. That is to say, they're essentially replicating patterns of trauma from their childhoods.

If we want to genuinely comprehend our inner child, we must learn to listen to and communicate in their sensory language. If you remember what life was like as a child, you'll remember that rather than speaking to you in full phrases, children will express their desires and needs to you by body language and intuitive noises. That is why a large part of reconnecting with our inner child is done by participation in activities that engage our entire range of senses. When we can be fully present instead of thinking our way through problems, we can access a space beyond our cognitive narrative. We have the opportunity to establish a new relationship with our inner child in our current life.

Reconnecting To Your Inner Child Through Activities

The strategies that have shown to be the most effective have been addressed extensively throughout this book, and they are summarized below. Record the activities you have finished and the influence they have had on your everyday life, no matter how minor the impact was.

☐ **Reestablish a connection with your childhood.**

One method of accomplishing this is to "time travel" back to your formative years. Make a list of the things that brought you joy when you were younger to help you with this process. This is the time to think and relive these recollections as though they were taking place right now.

Notes:

☐ **Identify your inner child archetype.**

As discussed in the first chapter, there are some patterns of inner child behavior that are shared by the majority of people. Examine which patterns ring true for you in order to gain insight into what is happening in your life right now. The following are some examples:

- The orphan child can appear as a result of not receiving enough attention from parents. A child's behavior can be relatively innocent, due to their parents' excessive workload, or it can be more severe, resulting from abuse or neglect.

- In adulthood, the eternal child is typically disregarded because he or she is healthy as a child. Do you recall a time when you were feeling playful and spontaneous, and having a good time without feeling guilty or anxious?

- The wounded child can appear for those who have experienced a great deal of criticism or suffers from worry on a regular basis when he or she does not receive adequate affirmation.

My inner child archetype is:

☐ **Write a letter to your inner child to express your feelings.**

If you believe you are living a life that does not honor your inner child, you can express your feelings by offering an apology. Alternately, you may send a brief letter to your inner child in which you explain that you aim to develop a closer relationship with your inner child in your current life.

With this strategy, you will inform your inner child that you are no longer interested in repeating the past. Write your letter to include all that you needed to hear as a child, whether it was affection and caring or a safe place to share your feelings.

You can also write it to your parents or guardians in the first person. It could go something like this:

- "You should have been given more opportunities to interact with kids your age instead of taking on adult responsibilities."
- "Play is an essential environment for children to develop, learn, and heal. My apologies for not giving you that opportunity."

When complete, read your letter aloud to help you process it more after you've written it. Alternatively, you might choose to read it while meditating on your own. To read this letter aloud, come up with a procedure that is comfortable for you.

Notes:

☐ **Monitor your feelings carefully.**

Your inner child has a lot of sensitivity and is therefore quite fragile. You must protect and nurture him or her. In order to connect with your inner child, it is critical to pay attention to the anxieties and insecurities that arise, as well as the joys and sensations of amazement that frequently arise when you connect with your inner child. Check in with yourself often throughout the day and ask, "How am I feeling right now?"

Notes:

☐ **Pay attention to your breathing and maintain a state of mindfulness.**

We can become more intrigued about the present by connecting with our deep breaths and physical body, which helps us move out of the responsibilities of adult life and reactive emotions. All five of our senses can be used to keep track of how we feel in the body. Taking three slow, deep breaths helps us relax. It may be beneficial to place one hand on your stomach and chest.

Notes:

☐ **Encourage your own individuality.**

It doesn't matter if we're allowing ourselves to do what we enjoy—whether it's drawing, cooking, gardening, sitting, or reading graphic novels—doing what we enjoy can be calming and restore us to our inner child.

Notes:

☐ **Gather anything of value.**

Do you remember what it was like to go about collecting stuff when you were a kid? It is possible to reconnect with our inner kid by collecting items that we come across on a walk or on our way to the beach (sticks, rocks or shells). We don't do this for any practical reason; rather, we do it for the pure enjoyment of it.

Notes:

☐ **Keep a journal.**

As previously discussed, the purpose of journaling is to provide a secure environment for you and your inner child to express yourself honestly, without the pressures of the outer world on your shoulders. It can take the form of simply sitting down and asking your inner kid how they're feeling on this particular day. The goal is to acknowledge and respect your inner child's assessment of their own experiences without filtering or changing their perception in any way.

Notes:

☐ **Take a look at or recreate photographs.**

Consider looking at old photographs of yourself as a child to remind yourself of any emotional scripts you may wish to rewrite. If you have suffered from neglect, it is probable that you will want to gaze at those photographs while murmuring quiet affirmations of love and protection to yourself.

Notes:

□ **Affirmations should be spoken aloud to your inner child.**

To help your inner child, re-examine positive affirmations that you believe will be helpful for them and post them around your room. Every morning, take a few minutes to repeat these affirmations out loud to yourself.

Here are some statements you can try:

- "I love you"
- "I'm sorry we had to go through that"
- "You deserve to be yourself"
- "You have the right to explore and play."
- "Your body is a comfortable place to be."

Notes:

□ **Begin therapy immediately.**

Getting in touch with your inner child might be a difficult endeavor. However, the good news is that you do not need to go it alone. Retracing your steps in the past and repairing your inner child may appear to be paradoxical at first glance. In other cases, however, when we find ourselves in a downward spiral, taking a step back is the most effective method to go forward to a place of healing.

Notes:

□ **Reminisce about your youth.**

Making nostalgic memories of your childhood is a wonderful approach to reconnect with your inner child. Try looking through photo albums and childhood diaries to get a sense of the past. It's possible that reminiscing with childhood friends and family members will help bring back memories that you'd entirely forgotten.

You can, however, come across painful memories when you go back over them. Inner child work is all about attempting to heal the emotional scars that have been left behind. This may entail discussing them with a close friend or family member, expressing them creatively, or talking about them with your psychotherapist.

Notes:

Finally, before we wrap off this chapter, here are a few thoughts to consider when it comes to dealing with your own inner child.

Final Questions To Consider

1. How does your inner child feel at the moment?
2. Describe anything you lacked or were deprived of as a child.
3. Is there a characteristic you possessed as a child that you cherish and wish you still had today?
4. What is it that your inner child is terrified of?
5. In what way does this have an impact on your life currently?
6. What would you say to your inner kid right now if you had the chance?

Conclusion

I want to take a moment to congratulate you on reaching the end of the book. I know that it may have been very difficult to read some of the information, and a lot of the scenarios that were described may have been all too familiar for you. I hope that you have gained a better understanding of how your inner child works and how to promote healing.

Throughout this book, you have learned how to communicate with your inner child and transform your life from being an impulsive reactor to becoming an authentic, aware creator.

In the first chapter, you learned what your inner child is and why connecting with them is beneficial. You also discovered the many archetypes of the inner child to better identify with the type that relates to you.

In the second chapter, you learned how abandonment anxieties manifest in adults and how they relate to the child within. You also discovered how alcoholic parenting affects our inner child, and how trauma can cause us to suffer emotional losses that are "under-the-surface". After that, you learned critical skills for reclaiming your inner child and healing your past traumas. In chapter three, you discovered how to communicate effectively with your inner child using tactics such as letter writing, affirmations, journaling, and more.

In chapter four, you learned how to get in touch with your shadow self to mend your inner child, as well as, embrace and address the more hidden facets of your personality. In the fifth chapter, you learned how to establish personal boundaries while also setting caring intentions for yourself.

You then discovered, in chapter six, how your inner child affects your most intimate connections. You learned that if you don't heal your inner child, it can become a hindrance in your relationships. You then discovered practical ways to jump-start the healing process and build stronger bonds with others.

In chapter seven, you learned that your inner child has an impact on your professional life. We discussed that when you have a wounded inner child, you develop personality traits that are unhelpful and might lead to difficulties in your career. You learned how to control these reactions and develop into a better performing individual.

In chapter eight, you discovered how to have a better understanding of your approach to finances and how it relates to parenting and your inner child. You discovered how to form new, more positive financial behaviors, which will help you break bad money habits.

When you reached chapter nine, you learned the value of journaling your inner child and received the most useful writing prompts for enhancing communication and healing. You were then provided with a breakdown of further activities that can be done to restore your injured inner child in the final chapter.

Now that you have finished this book, I want to leave you with this important point:

As you work on healing and getting to know your inner-child, remember to be patient and kind with yourself along the way. Everything you think and feel is correct. It can be exceedingly tough and frightening to speak up about a section of our lives that we have probably never given much thought to previously.

However, with time, you will discover that the majority, if not all, of the behaviors, thought patterns and beliefs you currently possess are a result of your early childhood experiences. It's basically everything about you, which is why getting to know your inner-child is so vital. Allow yourself plenty of time to do it. It's important to remember that you don't have to keep experiencing the pain. You have the ability to let go of the past and move forward to a more fulfilled life with loving relationships.

I wish you the best of luck on your journey to making a true connection with yourself and realizing the best you can become!

References

Association, A. P. (2021). *Getting Beyond Small Talk: Study Finds People Enjoy Deep Conversations With Strangers.* Getting beyond small talk: Study finds people enjoy deep conversations with strangers. https://phys.org/news/2021-09-small-people-deep-conversations-strangers.html.

Schoenfelder , E. (2011, January 1). *Quality Of Social Relationships And the Development Of Depression In Parentally-bereaved Youth - PubMed.* PubMed. https://pubmed.ncbi.nlm.nih.gov/20119668/.

Made in the USA
Monee, IL
09 September 2022

13576545R00057